STAR STEEDS AND OTHER DREAMS

THE COLLECTED POEMS
Dr Karl P.N. Shuker

Typeset by Jonathan Downes,
Cover and Layout by SPiderKaT for CFZ Communications
Using Microsoft Word 2000, Microsoft , Publisher 2000, Adobe Photoshop CS.

First published in Great Britain by CFZ Press

**CFZ Press
Myrtle Cottage
Woolsery
Bideford
North Devon
EX39 5QR**

© CFZ MMIX

All rights reserved. Without limiting the rights under copyright reserved above, no part of this publication may be reproduced, stored in or introduced into a retrieval system, or transmitted, in any form of by any means (electronic, mechanical, photocopying, recording or otherwise), without the prior written permission of both the copyright owners and the publishers of this book.

ISBN: 978-1-905723-40-9

DEDICATION

For my little blond-haired blue-eyed brother, André (27 October 1955 - 3 December 1955), whose passing four years before I was born meant that I could never share any of his short stay on Earth, or offer him a gift of anything, until now.

I have been a seeker of strange animals for many years as an adult, and also a writer of possibly even stranger verses, especially as a lean, mullet-haired, dream-headed youth – enthused with high hopes and even greater expectations for the future.

Whatever happened to that youth, I wonder, and whatever would André have thought of him? I hope with all my heart that he would have approved, and that he would have found pleasure in these poems.

We never met in this world, little bro, but, God willing, we shall meet in the next, and that will be truly wonderful.

PIC: The author with his West Highland white terrier puppy, Sam, back in 1981.

List Of Contents

Dedication	3
Introduction	9
Part 1 – What a Wonderful World	13
The Beautiful People	16-7
Dandelion Clocks	18
Fire	19
The Fly	20-1
A Memorial to the Passenger Pigeon	22-3
The Nightingale	24-5
The Praying Mantis	26-7
The Rose	28
The Star	29
Sunset, Sunrise	30-1
Swans and Horses	32-4
Through the Rainbow	35
The Tiger	36
Watching the Clouds	37

Part 2 – Other Worlds   39

The Awakening of Day   42
Dreams of Nature   43-6
Fire Pictures   47-8
The Ghost   49
Green Snake   50
The Mirror of Mnemosyne   51
A Phantasia of Ghosts and Illusions   52-3
Reflections in the Mirror   54
The Shadow   55
Sleep   56-7
Snow Dreaming   58-9
Starlight Fantasia   60-1
The Voice of the Winds   62-3
The Windmill   64
Worlds of Faerie   65

Part 3 – A Sense of Mystery   67

Ballet of the Willows   70-1
Behold the Thunder Horse   72-4
The Bomb   75-6
Fairy Lullaby   77
Flying Horse Fantasia   78-9
The Flying Saucer   80-1
The Haunted Cottage   82-3
The Loch Ness Monster   84
Oberon's Garden   85
Perchance a Mermaid?   86-7
The Pool of Dreams   88-9
The Star Horse   90-1
Stonehenge   92-3
Transforming The Dragon   94
A Tribute to Quetzalcoatl   95
The Unicorn / Dragons / Tattoos /
Mirabilis / The Panther   96-7

Part 4 – Looking Forward, Looking Back   99

Borne Into Tomorrow   102-3
A Call From My Past   104
The Clown   105
Dismissing Childhood   106
A Ghost From The Past   107

Patch – A Four-Legged Friend	108-9
Reflections of Summers Past	110-1
Remembering the Woodlands	112
Robin	113
The Rose Garden	114-5
The Scientists	116-7
The Silence of Solitude	118-9
A Silver Jubilee Tribute	120
Thoughts of a Dreamer	121
Yesterday's Street	122-3

Part 5 – The Glory of God   125

The Angel	128-32
As Bright as the Waterfall	133
The Christmas Donkey	134-5
Fields of Remembrance	136-7
Heaven's Bell	138-40
Here Comes Another Rainy Day	141
Life – The Infinity of the World	142-3
The Mole and the Fieldmouse	144-7
The Monastery Garden	148-9
The Music of the Spheres	150-1
The Robin and the Crossbill	152
The Swan of Tuonela	153
The Transformation of Saint Eustacius	154-6
What is God?	157
The Wild Roses	158
Wonders Untold	159

Part 6 – Younger Days   161

The Balloon	164
The Butterfly	165
The Church / The Churchyard	166
Fireworks – Bright Flowers of the Night	167
The Forget-Me-Not	168
The Mole	169
The Monastery	170-1
Mother Nature	172
Nod	173
Papillon	174
Polperro	175-7
The Puppy	178
The Weeping Willow Tree	179-80

White Star — 181

Part 7 – Time To Say Goodbye — 183

    Airport — 186
    And Forever Shall I Wait For You — 187
    Elvina — 188-9
    Endings — 190
    A Last Visit — 191
    The Last Morning — 192-3
    The Parting — 194
    Reborn — 195
    Worlds Apart — 196
    Yesterday No Longer – The Seashore By Twilight — 197

Index of Titles — 199

Acknowledgements — 203

About the Author — 205

Introduction
Time for a Rhyme

Poetry is the journal of the sea animal living on land, wanting to fly in the air. Poetry is a search for syllables to shoot at the barriers of the unknown and the unknowable. Poetry is a phantom script telling how rainbows are made and why they go away.

Carl Sandburg - *Poetry Considered*

It isn't always easy to remember when or how exactly a lifelong passion began, but as far as my undiminished love of poetry is concerned, I can date its origin precisely – to that magical, life-changing day when, as an 8-year-old child, my mother bought me a certain book. It was a wonderful anthology entitled *The Golden Treasury of Poetry*, containing over 400 poems selected by Louis Untermeyer, accompanied with delightful illustrations by Joan Walsh Anglund – and which I still own today, well-thumbed and a little dog-eared but as treasured now as it has always been. Until then, I had read various poems at school and had enjoyed them, but when confronted with hundreds of diverse, captivating verses on every conceivable subject all contained within the covers of a single book, I was totally spellbound.

Here, for the first time, I was introduced to such literary marvels as William Blake's 'Tyger, Tyger', Percy Bysshe Shelley's 'Ozymandias', John Keats's 'La Belle Dame Sans Merci', William Wordsworth's 'Daffodils', Alfred Noyes's 'The Highwayman', Sara Henderson Hay's 'The Shape God Wears', Christina Rossetti's ''Remember Me', W.B. Yeats's 'The Song of Wandering Aengus', Rudyard Kipling's 'If', Samuel Taylor Coleridge's 'Kubla Khan', the nonsense poems of Edward Lear and Lewis Carroll, the quirky nature poems of Emily Dickinson, the prefabulous animiles of James Reeves, and so much more. Soon I could recite many of them in the same easy way that I knew all of the words to my favourite songs, and I delighted in their rhythms and rhymes, in the evocative images conjured forth by their rich vocabulary, and in the ready escape to other worlds where their mesmerising words instantly transported me whenever I read them.

In short, my imagination was fired by poetry in a way that I had never experienced before, and, inevitably, it was not long before I began experimenting with writing poems myself. Much as I still enjoyed reading the verses of others, I now knew that this was no longer enough – I had to express in written form the rhymes and images that were welling forth in my head. And so, as an early teenager, I began to pen poetry in earnest, and continued doing so in prolific quantity until my early 20s. By then, however, other, more pressing literary demands had begun to require and receive my full attention, including university work and my first forays into freelance non-fiction writing. By the time that my first cryptozoological book and articles were published during the late 1980s, my poetry writing had all but ceased, and my folders of poems were tucked away in a bedroom bookcase, where they remained in quiet obscurity for more than two decades.

Just over a year ago, however, I noticed them there, took them out again, and began to read – and suddenly, the years simply melted away and I found myself remembering words that I had written so long ago that I had thought them forgotten forever. But no, they were still there, both on the page and in my memory, as if I had merely stepped outside for a moment and left the folders open on my desk, awaiting my swift return – a return that in reality had taken well over 20 years.

After painstakingly reading through every poem, I was not surprised to find that, with such an expanse of time separating the present day from the younger, bygone age when I had originally written them, some were very self-indulgent, and certain others less than technically adept (their youthful zeal notwithstanding). However, there were also a surprising number that seemed undiminished by the passing of time – but then, as their author, I suppose I would say that! Consequently, I handed out a number of these to a variety of friends and colleagues (including my agent Mandy Little of Watson, Little Limited in London), and at the risk of never speaking to them again should they be too acerbic in their responses, I asked them to comment unreservedly on whether they considered these poems worthy of publication.

Remarkably, I received an unequivocal affirmation from all concerned. Yes, they felt that these were indeed worthy of publication, and so, to cut a not-very-long story even shorter, when Jon Downes of the CFZ Press kindly expressed an interest in doing just that, the present book was born. Only a single modern-day poem of mine, penned just a few months ago, is included here – 'The Mirror of Mnemosyne', written specifically to explain what was at that time planned to be the book's title, but which has since been changed, to link instead with the delightful illustration used on the front cover. All of the others were originally penned during the mid-1970s to early 1980s (though a few of these have been modified slightly in more recent times). Moreover, as you will see, I have written on numerous subjects, in a variety of different styles, and there is one section devoted entirely to various poems that I have prepared specifically for children. You will also discover that personification of inanimate objects and concepts occurs frequently in my poetry, so look out for plenty of deliberate capitalisations, e.g. Time, Night, Eternity, etc.

One aspect of writing poetry that particularly appeals to me is the creation of word pictures, i.e. converting images and scenes into verbal descriptions. As a result, you will find that many of my poems are very descriptive in form, emphasising colours, movement, subtle changes of light, and other overtly visual facets of the world, and often have little storyline. I appreciate that this may not be to everyone's taste, but as this book contains the most personal, intimate writings of mine ever to have been published, these poems wholly embody my own writing style rather than adhering to one dictated or thrust upon me by any outside influence or convention.

For many people out there, especially those familiar with my cryptozoological writings, they may well assume that writing poetry is a new venture for me, a sequel of sorts to my non-fiction work or even a total departure, a new path taken by me leading away from my traditional publications. In reality, however, as you will now know having read this introduction (and which is the reason why I have written it in this explanatory, autobiographical style), my poetry is not a sequel but a prequel – that is, an early, pre-cryptozoological line of literary endeavour that was ultimately out-competed for my attention by my cryptozoological writings (although in my *Dragons* book I was able to revive to a certain extent my earlier, scientifically-unconstrained, imaginative style of writing when retelling various dragon-related myths and legends).

Had this not happened, who can say what I would have been writing today, what my previous publications (if any) would have been, and even what directions my entire life would have taken? In a sense, it is like speculating what route the evolution of life on earth would have taken if, for example, the mammalian lineage had been out-competed by some other animal group, or if the dinosaurs had not been annihilated by the end of the Cretaceous Period (cryptozoological examples excepted, of course!).

Anyway, such flights of speculative fancy aside, I am delighted to have received the opportunity to present at long last the first product of my 'other' line of literary evolution, resurrected from premature extinction and granted a life beyond the confines of some long-forgotten folders in a bedroom bookcase. I hope that you enjoy *Star Steeds and Other Dreams*, and that you will forgive any youthful over-exuberances, naivety, or precocity that you may encounter in it, and I thank you for your interest in experiencing this very different book of mine.

> The poet, as everyone knows, must strike his individual note sometime between the ages of fifteen and twenty-five. He may hold it a long time, or a short time, but it is then that he must strike it or never. School and college have been conducted with the almost express purpose of keeping him busy with something else till the danger of his ever creating anything is past.
>
> Robert Frost

PART 1:
WHAT A WONDERFUL WORLD

My poetry has been inspired by a myriad of different themes and subjects, but none more evocative and empowering than the glory and wonder of the natural world, and in particular the rich diversity of its wildlife.

>The little cares that fretted me,
>I lost them yesterday,
>Among the fields above the sea,
>Among the winds at play,
>Among the lowing of the herds,
>The rustling of the trees,
>Among the singing of the birds,
>The humming of the bees.
>
>The foolish fears of what might pass
>I cast them all away
>Among the clover-scented grass
>Among the new-mown hay,
>Among the hushing of the corn
>Where drowsy poppies nod,
>Where ill thoughts die and good are born –
>Out in the fields with God.
>
>Anonymous – 'Out in the Fields with God'

Above all others, we should protect and hold sacred those types, Nature's masterpieces, which are first singled out for destruction on account of their size, or splendour, or rarity, and that false detestable glory which is accorded to their most successful slayers. In ancient times the spirit of life shone brightest in these; and when others that shared the earth with them were taken by death they were left, being more worthy of perpetuation. Like immortal flowers they have drifted down to us on the ocean of time, and their strangeness and beauty bring to our imaginations a dream and a picture of that unknown world, immeasurably far removed, where man was not; and when they perish, something of gladness goes out from nature, and the sunshine loses something of its brightness.

>W.H. Hudson – *The Naturalist in La Plata*

The disturbing prospect that, despite our (allegedly) superior brainpower, humanity may now be further from God than are any of His other creations is the basis for this poem – a celebration of the purity and beauty of the wildlife all around us.

The Beautiful People

Blameless and fair are the infants of Nature,
Freed from Temptation and born without Care.
They are unblemished, untainted by Evil;
Mankind they heed not, for Eden is theirs –

Nature unparalleled, Beauty unending,
Radiant Kingdoms from which we are gone.
We were too weak, and Temptation destroyed us;
Fallen, we left, and were forced to pass on,

Lonely and shameful in exile unending,
Banished forever from that which was ours.
They were more wise, and sought only to follow
God and His Mercy, His Truth, and His Power.

Swallows skim brightly like throbbing pulsations
Soaring and gliding in infinite flight,
Rising forever through heavenly strata,
Shooting and streaming like spirits of Light.

Squirrels chase wildly through branches and treetops,
Russet infernos with flushes of flame,
Tails curling brightly like flickering candles,
Darting like fire in arboreal games.

Miniature harvest mice scurry through cornfields,
Tiny brown atoms of scampering joy;
Shyly inquisitive bundles of mischief,
Bustling with life like diminutive toys.

Mottled fawns lie 'neath the woodlands' green mantle,
Secretive denizens, peaceful and shy;
Perfectly camouflaged, dappled by Nature,
Watching her kingdom through dark wary eyes.

Mayflies flit gently like riverside sylvans,
Briefly they mate before sinking to die.
Short is their life, yet infused with rare beauty,
Born in the new when the old flutters by.

Thus they continue while mankind grows feeble,
Lovely they still are, and ever will be.
Fair and unchanging, the beautiful people,
They are His children – the wild, and the free.

Whenever I see a host of dandelion clocks gusting by in the breeze, I think of a whirling ballet of tiny dancers, twirling and spinning in a joyful celebration of nature, and of life itself, however brief it may be.

Dandelion Clocks

Like a fairy ballerina
Dancing softly through the trees,
Gliding silently through Summer
On the laughter of the breeze.

Waltzing gaily 'cross the meadows
As the hours just flutter by,
Twirling swiftly through the woodlands
Like a spotlight from the sky,

Pirouetting round their branches
In a cloud of gauzy dreams,
Rising gently through the shadows
On the sun's auroral beams.

Drifting long with other dancers
From this ballet of the trees,
Like a host of fairy stardust
Scattered far through fields and leas,

Till the heavens' sapphire summer
Is transformed to autumn grey.
Now they're gone, like cloudy snowflakes,
Having danced their lives away.

As Rudyard Kipling's 'Jungle Books' were among my favourite novels as a child (and still are today), I have little doubt that my floral metaphors for fire in this poem owe something to Kipling's animals referring to it as the Red Flower, a comparison that provides great scope for creative writing.

Fire

The bright flower of Evil, an orchid of flame,
The hot, scorching wingtip of Death,
Which vanquishes forests, and homesteads, and woods
With gusts of its venomous breath.

A flicker of crimson that blossoms and grows,
With petals that quiver and curl,
Which dazzles the eyes of the onlooking world
As its beauty it swiftly unfurls.

But touch not this shimmering creeper of Death,
A garland of scarlet and flame,
A glittering steed with a bright fiery mane,
And a temper that no-one can tame.

An omen of terror, a lustre of heat,
Whose plumes dart up faster and higher,
A dread, burnished lover whose passion ne'er ends,
For this is the fragrance of fire.

Although much of my poetry is of the rhyming variety, I have ventured from time to time into the less constrained world of prose, as with this composition.

The Fly

A vibrant whirring of wings filled the room, and I gazed up to see a large, bewildered fly whirling wildly round and round in dizzy, eccentric circles, periodically crashing into the deceptively transparent freedom of the windows, only to buzz around once more in unceasing, dazed convolutions.

"Kill it!" I thought, spearing it with dark, forbidding eyes like chilling sabres of death, as it spiralled above like a demented spirit drawn ever downward to damnation, pausing momentarily to wring its suckered appendages in expressionless despair.

But as my arm rose like a shadowed scythe of fear, the hopelessness of its plight enveloped me, and I sat back as if I were a lonely silhouette bowing before the inevitability of Fate, for I was stricken by the similarity of our twin existences.

Why, are we not from parallel worlds? You – from an outward macroworld, while I grope ever through an inward microworld. For I too am continually searching for the knowledge of my own fate, chasing alone through the endless channels and lonely corridors of my own mind, seemingly devoid of hope beneath such curtains of gloom, searching for that which eludes me, passing through empty chambers of nothingness.

This is my unknown, this is my Eternity – an eternity of hopeless dreams of fulfilment. A door lies open, a mirror lies within, and from its glass-illuminated interior a colourful circus clown gazes out. But the clown is weeping, for I myself am peering into the mirror – a mirror reflecting only my innermost feelings and beliefs.

And as I look, eyes bear down upon me, and faces appear. The world is watching, and waiting. People are murmuring, and raucous laughter surrounds me. Where am I to go? Only Fate can tell me. Yet I am unable to ask.

And so the world continues, the people turn away, finding some other source of amusement, while I am left to chase ever on through the phantoms of my own melancholia.

Thus my sympathy, little fly, is yours – we are both lost in alien worlds. Mine is of my own making, mine to endure. But yours may be replaced by your natural realm via my intervention, for yours I see through inward-reflecting mirrors, though you can never hope to see mine through your myriad-faceted orbs. Mine is yours inversely, and where they meet, there one day someone shall find the ultimate Truth.

So leave now, and forget the unforgettable. Why should we both suffer? Why should one stranger die by the hand of another?

I slowly arose again, almost as if I were a vast statue awakened from a deep sleep of petrification, and moved forward.

I raised my hand like a crescendo of silver trumpets, I opened the window and let the fly go.

When Martha Washington, a small grey dove-like bird, died in a cage at Cincinnati Zoo on 1 September 1914, her passing marked one of the most shameful episodes in the history of humankind – the extinction of the passenger pigeon, which, incredibly, had been just a century earlier the most abundant species of wild bird in the world, whose vast numbers as witnessed in enormous flocks migrating each year through the North American skies could be counted in the billions, until they were decimated by hunters. This poem is a tribute to that lost bird, and a stark reminder of the inconceivable wickedness responsible for its extermination. The final verse's last word, 'fly', deliberately breaks the tradition set throughout the poem of 'sky' being the last word in each verse, in order to underline a change of direction in the poem, from realism to mysticism.

A Memorial to the Passenger Pigeon

Each year, across the New World sky,
Would flocks of birds in millions fly –
Unending flights eclipsing light
While travelling through the sky.

Known as passenger pigeons, they –
The birds that hid the sun's bright ray
For days and nights while endless flights
Migrated through the sky.

But hunters saw this awesome sight
As food for sport in wild delight,
And shot to kill as ever still
More birds passed through the sky.

Huge raucous clouds of birds in flight,
All unsuspecting of their plight,
Were seen and shot, then left to rot,
As more soared through the sky.

The heavens filled with countless birds,
And through the lands their cries were heard,
As they flew past, upon their last
Migration through the sky.

The pigeons' flocks were soon reduced
When men with savage guns were loosed –
Who aimed and fired, and ne'er grew tired
Of shooting at the sky.

Dead birds grew greater every day,
But mankind's greed was swift to pay,
For soon, as feared, they disappeared –
No birds flew through the sky.

Then parties searched for any few
Survivors of those flocks that flew
Across the lands in mighty bands,
A-flying through the sky.

But none did any human find,
The victims of his brutal mind.
Extinct at last – the days were past
When flocks whirred through the sky.

At Cincinnati Zoo one day,
Poor lonely Martha passed away.
The last was dead, her soul was led
Across that boundless sky.

And only then did mankind weep,
A bitter harvest would he reap
For many years, as futile tears
Fell flooding from the sky.

But though their mortal days are done,
The pigeons' spirits linger on.
For up in Space, beyond man's face,
On silent wings they fly.

Down through the ages, much has been written about the beautiful song of this close relative of the blackbird and thrush, contrasting its rich voice with its drab plumage. Here is my own homage to the nightingale, shy philomel of the night.

The Nightingale

Drawn through the evening by strange haunting sadness
Glides a song glorious, richer than Love,
Lilting and blending in bubbling concertos,
Rising and falling, then drifting above,

Sung by a drab little minstrel of Evening,
Hidden away in the valleys of Night,
Small is his shadow, and sombre his plumage,
Soft are his feathers, and silent his flight.

Yet when his rich warbling notes ripple sweetly
Far through each woodland and dark country lane,
All stop to listen in breathtaking wonder,
'Ere this fair music grows fainter again.

Dulcet and sweet is the Song of the Evening,
Drawn from the caves of the lost and unknown,
Borne on the wing beats of swift, chilling breezes,
Past shapeless phantoms and up to the throne

Where – 'midst the Shadows of Life and Death hanging
Deep in suspensions of Time and of Space –
Night sits, serene in her mystical beauty,
Sable her image, and hidden her face.

Yet if her visage were shown for an instant,
Lit by the starlight, unveiled for a while,
We may perhaps see her wonderful beauty,
And glimpse in silence a solitary smile,

As she hears softly the Song of the Evening,
Borne from the depths of a cool country vale,
Telling of Beauty, of Love in the Highest,
Captured in song by the sweet nightingale.

Despite its small size, the praying mantis never fails to elicit within me a momentary thrill of icy shock and fear whenever I see one of these extraordinary, alienesque insects, with its mesmerising gaze and lethal pseudo-pious stance – all of which I have sought to encapsulate in the following poem.

The Praying Mantis

There it squats – Death's fearful gargoyle –
Like a monster cast from Space;
Eyes unblinking stare in silence
From its strange, hypnotic face
Like a pair of shining gemstones –
Glinting facets, cold but bright –
Gleaming softly 'midst the shadows
With a pale, unearthly light.

Here it waits amongst the leaflets
In a pious, praying stance,
Yet the burning fires of Evil
In those deathless orbs still dance
As this prayerful gorgon crouches
In an alien repose,
And its eyes, ne'er closing, flicker,
Each a fiery, blood-tipped rose.

Hush! A movement flutters downwards –
There, a small, unwary fly,
Flitting closer, ne'er perceiving
How it all too soon will die.
For within a second's lifetime,
Moving faster e'en than Thought,
Flick-knived forelegs take it captive;
And the battle has been fought.

Soon it waits again, unnoticed,
'Midst the shadows of the trees,
With intelligence so chilling
That the very sun would freeze
If this ghoul e'er gazed upon it
In the glory of the skies.
None but Death may find a shelter
In those cold, unblinking eyes.

The poetry of the mystic William Blake has enriched my life for many years, and it inspired me greatly when I sought to embody in mere words the sumptuous, passionate beauty of what must surely be the world's most alluring flower.

The Rose

Who made thee, displayed thee –
Enrapturing starlet?
A crimson inferno
'Midst flushes of scarlet.
With bright inflorescence
Like vivid fluorescence,
Who cast, ne'er surpassed thee –
Most perfect of all?

Who blessed thee, possessed thee –
Enchanting suffusion?
More lovely, more fragrant
Than any illusion.
Intensely desiring,
A lustre untiring,
Surviving and thriving
When all others fall.

Who placed thee, embraced thee
'Midst kingdoms of mortals?
Whose sunbeams caress thee
From Heaven's bright portals?
For Beauty you nourish,
And thus will you flourish
Fore'er more, until your
Creator will call.

The scientist inside my brain tells me that stars are colossal conflagrations of fiery gas burning in the depths of Outer Space untold millions of miles away, but the poet within my mind prefers to liken them to delicate flowers blooming in the evening sky overhead, or to fragile candles doomed to be extinguished by the coming of day.

The Star

Like an eye through Dark's veiled shadow
Shines a frosty-petalled star,
In a bed of hazy aura.
O'er a sleeping world afar.

Twinkling softly through the silence
Of the solitudes of Night,
Ever watching, as its fragrance
Fills the countryside with light

Like a shining flower of Heaven
From the valleys of the sky,
Till the morning's beams perceive it,
And once more doom it to die

In the burning streams of glory
From the sun's resplendent gaze,
As it wilts with lonely sadness
In a pale, pellucid haze.

But when Evening rises slowly
From the hillsides of the past,
It is born again, unblemished,
Through the dusky light to last,

Like a candle burning brightly,
Till the silhouette of Day
Spies this fragile, twilit fairy
And blows softly it away.

Surely the most spectacular sights in all of Nature are the setting and the rising of the sun, torching the skies aflame with its fiery glory as it sinks downwards to die before reappearing in resplendent triumph amid the glowing heavens.

Sunset, Sunrise

Like a golden shadow drifting
Down the corridors of Night,
Like a glowing, saffron planet
Moving past the worlds of Light,

Gliding downwards through the evening,
Past the galaxies of stars,
Past the fairy rings of Saturn,
And the burnished face of Mars.

Floating down on cloudy cushions
Hanging through the roseate skies,
Interspersed by stars that twinkle
Like a host of fireflies.

Down and down the sun sinks slowly,
To the sleeping waves and sea,
Past the shadows of the evening,
Down through all Eternity,

To the hush of bygone mornings
In the realms of dreams and sleep,
Where trees whisper through the ages,
And bright fountains softly weep,

Till the dawn with vivid brush-strokes
Paints the waking morning sky.
Then the ghosts of empty eons
Through the heavens slowly fly

In a hazy mist of star moths,
Past the mountains white with snow,
To worlds far beyond our knowing,
Where forget-me-nots still grow.

But the sun stirs slowly, gleaming
Through the drowsy clouds of grey,
Rising softly up once more, to
Greet the brimming newborn day

Like a fiery horse of Heaven,
Racing through the skies so wide.
Who would dare this steed to harness?
Who would dare the sun to ride?

What might happen if a flock of swans somehow coalesced with a herd of horses, even if only in a half-dreaming mind? That intriguing premise was the starting point for the following word-picture – a poetical flight of imagination...in every sense!

Swans and Horses

Like a phalanx borne from Heaven
On a golden drift of Love
Glides a stream of snowy shadows
From the cloud-worlds far above
In an ever-wider spiral
Sweeping slowly through the skies,
While the lake's reflection shimmers
Like a star within their eyes,
Growing brighter every second
As their silhouettes descend
To its violescent waters,
Where the ripples softly wend –
Each a trembling ring of sunlight
'Ere it falls away to die,
Just an iridescent nimbus
'Neath a cerulean sky.

Now the swans reside serenely
Near the sable-mantled shade
Of the melancholy willow
From the lakeside's dappled glade,
Where the breezy zephyr murmurs
As its gusty whispers cool
Catch the willow's pearly teardrops,
Each a tiny silvered pool
Cast in deep, despondent sorrow
As the willow bows in grief,
Dewdrops trickling down in torrents
From each slender yellow leaf.

Here the swans glide by in silence,
Necks held high in regal stance
As their eyes gaze up to Heaven
While its darting sunbeams dance
Through their incandescent plumage,
Wings held proudly o'er their back
Like an arch of sparkling crescents
Tipped with inky plumes of black.
On they glide, past ruffling meadows
Flecked with starry trains of flowers,
Blooming brightly in the shelter
Of their viridescent bowers.

And across these speckled grasslands
To the silver-spangled streams
Chase a herd of snowy horses
Like a host of starlit beams,
Manes caressed by breezy fingers,
Like a sea of moonlit waves
Surging down across their shoulders
From its underwater cave,
As their eyes, afire and glowing,
Burn with bright undying flame,
While their tails toss ever skyward
With a joy that none can tame.

Soon they pass from sight and being
'Neath the woodlands' leafy shade,
And my eyes grow weak and heavy,
Each with slumber overlaid.
Yet as Hypnos murmurs softly
From the drowsy realms of Sleep,
Still the horses race before me
As their flowing spirits leap
'Cross the streams and to the lakeside
Where the swans sedately gaze
Through the heavens' golden shadow,
Through the skies' translucent haze

And as clouds float by in silence
O'er the warm, caressing skies,
Strange to say, the swans and horses
Merge as one before my eyes –
And as Morpheus casts softly
Dreams of slumber round my mind,
Wingèd steeds ascend to Heaven,
Leaving lake and streams behind.
Wings spread forth, and lustrous feathers
Gleam and glow like rays of light,
As these fair, enchanted visions
Pass so swiftly from my sight
To their mellow hierarchy
That no man shall ever see.
Earth is ours – a world of mortals.
Theirs is Immortality.

The spectacular, vivid spectrum of colours filling every corner of our world must surely be one of the greatest gifts that anyone can enjoy. I have always been fascinated by how this multitude of shades and hues can be expressed in words as well as by visual means, and there is surely no greater challenge than to capture and celebrate the polychromatic wonder of the rainbow within the medium of the written word. That, therefore, became my goal with this poem, to create my own vibrant multicoloured rainbow in rhyme

Through the Rainbow

Upwards I glide through a brilliant archway
Spanning the chasms of Space far above,
Sewn by the radiant needle of Heaven –
Weaving its splendour from sunbeams of Love.

Upwards and on through its crystalline crescents,
Casting a multihued shadow of Light,
Lost in a world of reflecting translucence
Showering colour in shimmering flight.

Upwards forever in vivid crescendos
Streaming like fountains through lilac-lit skies,
Swiftly ascending in bright sapphire spirals –
Sparkling like diamonds in star-showered eyes.

Upwards and onwards through whirling suffusions
Blushing like crimson-tipped roses of fire,
Passing through arches of amber and turquoise
Curving through Space like celestial lyres.

Upwards I soar through this arcuate spectrum
Spraying forth shaftlets of sun-shattered rays –
Rocketing outwards in golden aurorae
Filling the heavens with glistening haze.

Upwards, e'er upwards, like amethyst arrows
Bursting asunder with petals of flame,
Riding forever the arcs of the rainbow;
Light is my spirit, and Colour my name.

Tigers have always fascinated me, but I was only too aware that any attempt to capture this great cat's beauty and power in verse would be fraught with the peril of comparison with William Blake's spellbinding 'Tyger Tyger'. Nevertheless, eventually the lure of challenge became too great, and the following poem is my own tribute to this most magnificent, and terrifying, of creatures.

The Tiger

Deep in the primeval fires of the cosmos
Death was released from his shimmering tomb,
And as they danced in the dawn of Creation
Death bore a child from the flames of their womb.

You were that child, spawned by Death's great Inferno,
Hidden on Earth 'neath his Shadow of Fear,
Shrouded by Night until Heaven sent sunlight,
Then, by its silhouette, did you appear.

Who could have known that such beauty held terror
Deep within radiant emerald eyes,
Wrought and emblazoned in Death's blazing furnace,
Dewdrops of fear like the tears that you cry?

Space cannot hold you, and Time dare not chain you,
None can oppose you in glittering might.
Ebony ripples lash amber resplendence,
Scorning the shame of the sun's feeble light,

Scorching through Night like a firebrand of crimson,
Shredding the skies with each thunderous breath.
Yet, though so splendorous, e'er are you deadly,
Chilling in form, for your beauty is Death.

Who hasn't stared up at the sky, and in their imagination transformed the clouds floating by into all manner of images – dragons, horses, faces, and countless other forms? Sometimes, however, clouds remind me of ghosts – silent phantoms stealing across an empty stage before vanishing from sight.

Watching the Clouds

Silver ghosts of silent skies,
Moving softly, phantomwise,
Through the planes of wind and space,
Freckles on the sky's blue face.

Snowy-white in weightless ease,
On they float o'er lands and seas,
Through the realms of Space and Time,
Past dark lands and worlds sublime.

Changing shape and size they sail,
Leaving neither path nor trail,
Moving onwards, roaming free,
Through unseen Eternity.

And when Evening draws its veil
'Cross the globe, still on they sail,
Round the sun as down it sinks;
Now they're mauve, and flushed with pink.

So they leave, with tips of fire,
Over seas of bright sapphire,
Darkened now till Dawn's release,
Downy clouds on wings of Peace.

PART 2:
OTHER WORLDS

There are other worlds everywhere – worlds of Space and Time, mirror worlds and shadow worlds, worlds of sleep and starlight, fire and phantoms, snowfall and death, and the myriad inner worlds of the imagination. Journey with me now into some of my own worlds, far from those of the dreary waking day.

> To see a world in a grain of sand
> And a heaven in a wild flower,
> Hold Infinity in the palm of your hand
> And Eternity in an hour.
>
> William Blake – 'To See a World'

All of us beings here are cells of the unknown essence of our world, nodes of flesh that could as well be notes of melody. We are part of something infinite and eternal. There is no boundary between us and the world. In a profoundly relative sense, each of us may simultaneously occupy that particular focal point through which the entire universe is singing at this moment.

Are we then God's dream set to music in the place where the sea and the wind have begun to awake and think? Grateful for our blessing, even when they hurt, we trust the world is not paining needlessly for our sweet incertitudes 'twixt desire and reason. We would wish to be wiser and more loving, but for good or ill, our memories are young in this ancient oasis. And we comprehend little. How indeed could a part hear the Whole, or a note the Melody?

Yet the silence of space that enwombs the earth is not totally void. Indeed it is now revealed to be latent, pregnant, mystic — even as it was in the beginning that had no beginning — even as it will be in the end that can have no end. For this is the secret of the spirit that is the life of the form that is the language of the spirit — the eternal spirit that somewhere, somehow, found its voice, took wing and came alive.

Guy Murchie – *The Seven Mysteries of Life*

This poem was penned by me as an exercise in personification, imagining all of the major elements – the dawn (Eos), sky, sun, moon, stars, evening, sleep, and day – as living entities, making their entrances and exits in Shakespearean grandeur upon the ultimate stage, Heaven

The Awakening of Day

Silently, Eos rekindles her candle,
Sending forth slowly each flickering ray,
Snaring the stars as they twinkle in slumber –
Caught unaware by the heralds of Day.

And as the sky draws its shimmering curtain
Back 'cross the dark, empty windows of Night,
Swiftly the sun casts its soft, cloudy blankets
Far through the heavens in ripples of light,

Yawning, as Sleep glides unseen from his bedside
Back to her valley of wandering dreams,
Then rising proudly through radiant Heaven,
Painting the morning with glistening beams,

Showering all with a fountain of sunlight,
All but the moon draped in shadows of grey,
Silently mourning the exile of Evening –
Banished from Space by the coming of Day.

Bidding farewell, like a frail agèd spinster,
Leaving at last her celestial home,
Passes the moon 'cross the heavens' bright archway,
Ending beneath Twilight's crystalline dome.

There she will rest, till the sun's golden shadow
Drips from the sky in a puddle of grey.
Then like a ghost will the moon rise in glory,
Called into life by the cortège of Day.

I wrote this poem as a paean of praise to Nature – and, indeed, to Supernature, even Ultranature, perfect Nature beyond humanity's normal sensory perceptions – and to its glory through all eternity, as personified by Perpetua.

Dreams of Nature

Through sleepy vales of pastel green
I passed, one Summer morning;
'Neath dreaming skies of blissful blue
Reborn with Daylight's dawning,
While faraway the ocean's roars
Still echoed long from silent shores.

And on I strolled, 'neath golden clouds,
Past dancing, crystal fountains
That leapt and sang in sparkling joy
From lilac, snow-capped mountains
Like diamond stars with lucent glee,
And blessed by Immortality.

And through the skies the sun was drawn
By two emblazoned horses
That raced along a burnished trail –
Two crimson, fiery forces
With streaming tails like scarlet lyres,
And scorching eyes like dancing fires.

Still on I passed through glades of trees –
Tall, silver dendroids gleaming
Like astral arcs with spangled boughs,
And fragrant flowers beaming,
Pulsating light in fragile streams
Like cloudy, half-forgotten dreams.

Ah, Nature! Truly thou art here,
Amidst thine own perfection,
In this, thy world of unborn dreams,
For who could give correction
To this, thy realm, and thine alone,
Which Time's own seeds could not have sown.

And meadows flecked with sleeping flowers
Lay far into the distance –
For Nature gave them love of Life,
The will for their existence –
Exuding sweet, enchanting scent
That zephyrs' drifting murmurs sent

Across the cerulean hills
To kiss the mauve reflections
Of pool and lake in lilac groves,
Translucent, clear perfections,
Each rippling long, with violet torqued,
As turquoise swallows skimmed and hawked.

And here I see thou dwellest too,
Perpetua, my dearest,
Whose eyes reflect the vales of Space
Like pools of beauty clearest.
For here thou too can seek release,
For here alone thou findest Peace.

Ah, Peace! I see thy figure bright –
A slender, tranquil maiden
Amidst the elvish vales and woods,
All intricately laden
With gauzy webs of spider-thread
In rippling green and blushing red.

So look into the western skies
And see her shadow shining –
A smiling face with deep blue eyes
As pure as Heaven's lining.
And there, amid the clouds above,
A Sign is born – a snowy Dove.

Perpetua – all knowest thee –
Celestial, immortal –
Who passes e'er through Space's door,
Through Time's eternal portal,
To other worlds concealed from all,
Till all receive the Shining Call.

And from the rainbow's golden end
The souls of Colour fluttered
In evanescent cloudy drifts,
As ageless mountains muttered
'Neath shattered brows of crumbling stone,
As old and pale as whitened bone.

And all around lies Space, supreme –
A vacuum dark, unending –
Which bore thee once, Perpetua,
To send thy spirit wending
From wells of Time to strange new worlds
Where dormant Life would be unfurled.

And so, as star steeds raced in joy
Across their twinkling haven,
I took my leave of Nature's bliss
'Neath darkened mountains graven.
For Time is swifter still, it seems,
And past are all my Nature dreams.

For now I wake, once more alone
Amidst my own surrounding.
Yet still within my sleepy eyes
The star steeds' souls are bounding.
And still, Perpetua, I see
Thee shining far ahead of me.

Yea, ever will I see thy face
Before my life's ambition,
As e'er wilt thou personify
My lifetime's expedition,
Till I no more this world shall see,
For, yea, thou art Eternity.

Who hasn't stared into the bright flickering flames of a fire and imagined all manner of ever-changing sights portrayed by their savage yet beautiful dance?

Fire Pictures

Amid the fire's auroral glow
Lie far-off realms of long ago,
Recaptured now in crimson hues
With violet tints and smoky blues.

Imagination often takes
My searching eyes past amber lakes
Where groves of scarlet forests sway
'Midst scorching, incandescent rays.

And golden steeds with flaming manes
Race endlessly o'er burnished plains,
While hidden 'neath the fiery skies
Prowl lions bold, with ruby eyes.

And conflagrating dragons roar,
While streaming bolts of lightning pour
From seething nostrils, tongue, and heart,
And from their jaws flames curl and dart.

Emblazoned chateaux rise through clouds
'Midst burning willows downward-bowed,
And through the coruscating skies
The iridescent phoenix flies.

But soon, before my dazzled eyes,
Each splendid vision fades and dies,
Until no flame eruptions spout;
For all is gone – the fire is out.

Yet hidden from my silent eyes,
Like unseen candles through the skies,
The souls of Fire flit on in Space
To other worlds beyond my face.

And there, perhaps, another child
Will witness their enchantment wild,
And see himself, in flickers curled,
The mystic lands of Fire unfurled.

When writing, I often find myself returning to certain themes and motifs – mirrors and reflections, shadows and phantoms, parallel worlds, the past and future uniting, solitude, silence, and God. All of these, and more, can be found here.

The Ghost

Who stands 'neath the eaves draped in shadows?
Who dwells 'midst the darkness of Night?
Who calls with a whisper of pathos,
In sorrowful, meaningless flight?

"I stand – 'midst the dusk of the evening;
I call – from the far side of Time;
I flit – 'midst the valleys of Sadness,
Rhyme lacking in reasonless rhyme.

"I call – I alone, I unnoticed
In Morning's pale sun-shadowed dawn.
I call – from the noontide's bright wonder,
As I through all kingdoms am borne.

"I dwell 'midst a grey world of Shadow
E'erlasting, past all mortal sight –
A parallel world, silhouetted
In pools' depthless doorways of Light.

"And here you may see me reflected –
A phantom transparent in Space.
And in your eyes, Memory-painted,
Look inward to witness my face –

"A face from the Past and the Future,
Recaptured and borne into being –
A shadow – till stand I unblemished,
An infant before the All-Seeing."

Our innermost emotions can assume many forms, but, hopefully, none as tangibly malevolent as the version described here – ophiophobes, look away now!

Green Snake

Well I know you, gleaming Green Snake,
Brightly wrapped in shining mail.
Well I know your silent movement,
Gliding forth on glinting scales,

To your unsuspecting victim
Sleeping peacefully in bed,
As your forked tongue whispers softly
Through the dreams that fill his head.

Now your coils enfold him tightly
In a feverish embrace,
And a potent stream of venom
Drips like fire upon his face

As your toxic tongue still murmurs
Like a wind through silent leaves,
Infiltrating his subconscious,
Till inside his mind it weaves

Webs of Doubt and Greed and Envy,
Soon eclipsing Love and Bliss,
Turning Beauty into Hatred –
Strong and deadly is your kiss.

And when morning comes, your victim
Rises full of Rage and Spite,
Hurting others with his cruelty,
Setting Love and Peace alight

By the flame of Hate inside him
That one day, his heart, will take.
Yes, I know you well of old – for
You are Jealousy, Green Snake.

In Greek mythology, Mnemosyne was the mother of the nine Muses, and was also the personification of memory. But just how accurate, how reliable, are our memories? For when we look back at our life, how much of what we remember is real, and how much is what we'd have liked it to have been?

The Mirror of Mnemosyne

Dark, still, enshadowed, the mirror of Mnemosyne,
Moonlight encircling its chill, quicksilvered face.
Standing beside it, the masked goddess of Memory,
Ageless, all-seeing, transcending time and space.

Dare for a moment to gaze into her looking-glass,
See what you may in its crystalline mirage,
Brimming with happiness, hope, despair, and tragedy,
Each mood reflected upon its pale visage.

Do not anticipate viewing your own imagery,
Nor will your past be recaptured and displayed.
All you will see is the sum of your remembrances,
Rose-tinged distortions, each summoned and replayed.

These are your yesterdays, edited and modified,
Transformed by memory, shaped and cast anew.
Now just as real as the past itself had ever been,
Dreams become history, tangible and true.

So, as you linger, your captive eyes still mesmerised,
Drawn through the depths of the mirror's sable pool,
Who can be sure that the past is not a fantasy,
Mocking our minds like the laughter of a fool?

The following poem owes its creation to a very curious snatch of conversation that I happened by chance to overhear one day on the radio, in which the speaker was contemplating whether it might be that many of the people that we casually pass by without interaction or see only from a distance are nothing more than ghosts, mere phantoms. And so, from this remarkable muse, sprang 'A Phantasia' (constituting, incidentally, the longest single sentence to appear in any of my writings!).

A Phantasia of Ghosts and Illusions

Hear the echo of a lifetime
Doomed forever more to last,
Or a murmur drifting backwards
From the theatres of the past,

Whirling softly through a vortex
Spinning deep in silent Space
Like a whirlpool in the heavens,
Or an eye within a face

Gazing outwards, yet unseeing,
Pale as Dawn's auroral birth
From the snowy dreams of slumber
Shrouding velvet, verdant Earth,

Like an unseen clock vibrating
As its lifetime ebbs away,
While its fingers trace the seconds
Of another unborn day

Through the silhouettes cast downwards
From the shadows of the stars,
Now a host of winging phantoms
From a distant world afar,

Flitting slowly through the evening
As the planets e'er rotate,
Each a windmill in a spiral
On a shining, spangled plate

Spinning outwards e'er to nowhere
In their orbit round their lord,
While lugubrious crescendos
Chase like half-forgotten chords

In a lonely helter-skelter
Through the avenues of Time;
They – the spheres' eternal music –
Lacking syllables or rhyme,

Drifting downwards through the starlight
Lest their meaning fades away
To a ghost upon the moorlands
Of an evanescent day

Ever seeking 'midst the future
For a future of its own,
As the souls of Past and Present
Soar like cloudlets to the throne

Of a duplicated kingdom
On Time's unknown, farthest side,
Where their memory still lingers,
Round its universe to glide,

While they merge with more illusions –
None is real, for none can be
In this pseudo-world of Shadow
Cast from vacant Destiny

Like a set of footprints chasing
After footprints of their own,
Or a pool's encircling ripples
Running rings around a stone;

Yet their messengers are present
In a hundred other lands,
Groping ever through their darkness
Like a metamorphic hand,

E'en within our crowded suburbs
'Midst their noisy, raucous hosts,
Who could guess that most are shadows,
Mindless images, just ghosts?

Mirrors have always fascinated me, confronting me with my other self, exact but reversed, and showing me a glimpse of their replicate world – as real as my own, and, who knows, perhaps even more so?

Reflections in the Mirror

I am me, and you are also.
Am I you, or are you me,
As we gaze, each seeming brighter,
Into deep Eternity?

And your mirror world shines softly
With a cool quicksilver light
As your searching eyes call ever
For my spirit's silent flight

Through the mirror's timeless border
To the other side of Space,
Where my world is yours reflected
In the mirror's glossy face.

All stands still in ageless wonder
As my world just flutters by
Like a phantom caught by daylight
In the glowing eastern sky.

But I enter not this kingdom –
The inversion of my own.
Yet I stand before the mirror
Like an image lost, alone,

And my other calls me softly
Through the mirror's sparkling hue
As I gaze, and still I wonder,
Are you me, or am I you?

What happens to our shadow when we sleep? Does it lie hidden amid the darkness of other shadows, awaiting our awakening, or does it depart for adventures of its own amid Night's secret dominions? Ever since I first read Hans Christian Andersen's enthralling but chilling story 'The Shadow' as a youngster, I have always been intrigued, by that niggling thought.

The Shadow

Here I walk and you walk also,
Long you've travelled by my side,
Dark and mystical as Evening,
Through whose cryptic lands you glide

When I slip in silent slumber
From your world of starlit Night.
Then you too, in unseen swiftness,
Travel far in darkened flight

To the sombre Night-time nations,
Past each moonlit tree and glade,
Where the veiled domains of Evening
To your form become displayed,

As you pass by lonely islets
In the seas of Dark and Gloom,
While the misty ghosts of Evening
Through the sable valleys loom.

For your world lies deeply hidden
From the sunlight's dancing beams,
In the phantom realms of Evening,
And the secret world of Dreams.

I am Light, and you are Darkness;
I am Day, and you are Night.
Yet remain we close together,
Still within each other's sight;

And will be, until my leaving
For another World afar.
Then beyond my sight you'll vanish,
'Neath the shadow of the stars.

Much has been written about the scientific and philosophical associations between sleep and death, but the ancient Greeks encapsulated these links in a particularly telling, succinct manner via personification. For in classic Greek mythology, death is a god called Thanatos (not to be confused, though he often is, with Hades, god of the Underworld), and is the twin brother of Hypnos, god of sleep, with Morpheus, god of dreams, as the son of Hypnos. Moreover, the parents of Thanatos and Hypnos are none other than Nyx (Night) and Erebos (Darkness). In addition, one of the most famous death-related scenes in Greek mythology is the passage across the River Styx to the Underworld of the boat steered by Charon the silent ferryman and filled with the souls of the dead. Consequently, to emphasise the ancient Greeks' perceived kinship between death and sleep, I chose to adapt the latter boat scene, transforming it from one that features the dead to an equivalent featuring sleepers and sleep (though as a female rather than male personification), but acknowledging the link between sleep and death by way of the final verse.

Sleep

Day sinks away through the oceans of Evening,
Rippling like stars sweeping outwards to die,
While from their vortex the moon rises softly,
Borne from its depths to the roof of the sky.

And 'cross the waters a boat glides serenely,
Nod is its helmsman, and Sleep is its queen.
Gently it drifts o'er the waves deep in slumber,
Dappled in shadows of violet and green.

Grey are the sails, each dream-woven by Twilight,
Sewn from the cobwebs that Morning passed by;
Pale is its image 'neath moonlit aurorae,
Fashioned from memories, murmurs, and sighs.

And from its silhouette Sleep whispers gently,
Calling to mortals who follow like shades –
Entering slowly her boat of enchantment,
Drawn through the evening to mystical glades

Deep in the depths of the hidden subconscious,
'Neath the dark heavens of shimmering Night –
Silently watching her star-shadowed journey
Into the morning, 'ere fading from sight.

Waves bear Sleep calmly through dream-clouded kingdoms,
Misty surroundings of lilac and grey,
Fragile illusions like butterfly wing beats,
Melting like ghosts 'neath the lantern of Day.

And as the dawn blushes shyly through Heaven,
Far 'cross the ocean is Sleep softly borne,
Each mortal soul drifting back to its dwelling,
Waking once more to the laughter of Morn.

Thus she continues – the wisest immortal –
Fair both in features and mind she'll remain,
Leading our souls till the world calls no longer,
Then shall we never look homeward again.

One of the most mesmerising figures in fantasy literature must surely be the Snow Queen as conceived by Hans Christian Andersen. Here is my tribute to the alluring, illusive kingdom of snow and its bewitching, pitiless monarch.

Snow Dreaming

A wilderness, white and unending,
Lay waiting, my soul to enfold,
As softly its slim, chilling fingers
Froze even my whispers with cold.

Its shimmering mantle draped slowly
My ankles with starflakes of snow,
While winds from the chateaux of Winter
Sent billowing murmurs of woe

Through clouds each suspended from Heaven
O'er landscapes enveloped in white,
As faintly a polar sun flickered –
A candle of shivering light.

And ever the icicles glittered,
Like pendants transparent and cool,
And ever the visage of Winter
Laughed softly through crystalline pools,

While snowflakes drew pale, bitter petals
O'er window, and garden, and door,
As slowly my steps led me onwards,
But only a nothingness saw.

For grimly the blizzard lashed downwards –
A phantom as chilling as Death –
As ever I strove to avoid it,
To turn from its glacial breath.

But Winter's pale wraiths sang out softly,
And slowly their song drew me on,
Till, howling, the winds quelled their music,
And when I looked up, they were gone.

Yet there, in their stead, just beyond me,
The Snow Queen stood, calling my name.
To struggle was futile, was useless,
As ever approaching she came.

Her arms stretched out glowing towards me,
Enticing me nearer to Doom,
As, frozen, my spirit lay dormant –
A ghost in a windowless room.

Her eyes laughed in terrible silence,
Cold diamonds of shimmering blue.
And closer I stumbled towards her,
As stronger her influence grew,

Till spectres of snow loomed all round me
Like phantasms shapeless and pale,
Enshrouded in misty grey mantles,
And spangled with gemstones of hail.

Then softly a Voice spoke beyond them:
"Walk on – to your world, and your home."
The sun shone forth strongly above me,
A beacon from Heaven's bright dome.

And when I looked onwards, the Snow Queen
Grew wan in the sun's holy light
Until, like a great mournful shadow,
Her form passed away from my sight.

And silence once more lay behind me,
Retracing my vanishing track.
And ever the sun led me onwards.
And nothing again called me back.

Here is a word-picture poem revealing a silver-hued fantasy realm of starlight, far removed in space and time from our own mundane world. So let your imagination take wing for a while, and leave the cares of our sad little planet far behind.

Starlight Fantasia

Like a sphere of icy moonlight,
Like a spool of shrouded snow,
Lies a world in sparkling starlight,
Turning softly, far below,

In its orbit through the heavens,
Gliding on as e'er it moves
Round its sleepy sun in wonder,
Drawn through unseen astral grooves.

Birds more lovely than a rainbow
Dart beneath its shadowed trees,
And the sylphs with gauzy mantles
Float upon the evening breeze.

And throughout the misty heavens
Swans and horses swiftly fly,
Down beneath the dappling moonbeams
Where the planets journey by.

And the mottled trees of night-time
Whisper melodies of grace,
But their songs are those of ages,
Spanning lifetimes, worlds, and Space.

Silver pools of starlit sadness
Ripple on through countless hours,
While soft music rises upwards
From the evening's blooming flowers –

Calling through the planes of stardust,
Through a universe of stars,
Answered by a thousand minstrels
From another world afar.

Sapphire swallow calls to swallow
O'er the spider-webs of Time,
And a hundred thousand bluebirds
Sing with dulcet tones sublime.

Still the planets circle softly
'Midst the sable cloak of Night,
Calling softly, ever calling,
Through the shimmering starlight,

Like a thousand ghostly murmurs,
Like a hundred ringing chimes,
Like great butterflies they move through
Silent corridors of Time.

Only they have learnt the secret
That no thing is what it seems,
Just illusions, simply shadows,
In an everlasting dream.

And when Dawn arises slowly
Out of Evening's cavern deep,
Mystery flies softly westward
To the spiralled realms of Sleep.

And when we slowly awaken,
We know not of what is past,
Of the haunting worlds behind us,
Which forever more will last,

Till the shining, gleaming planets,
Softly dying, fade to grey.
And then we will know their secret,
As we slowly fly away.

Two very different poems of mine owe their origin to an extraordinary, surreal painting by René Magritte. Entitled 'The Voice of the Winds', it depicts three enormous, alien-looking spheres floating ominously above a rural scene. Whereas one of my poems, 'The Music of the Spheres' (included in Part 5 of this present collection), was directly influenced by that compelling image, the other poem, presented below, focuses instead upon the painting's very evocative title.

The Voice of the Winds

Dark the forest lay, silent and sombre,
In Morning's first saffron-lit rays,
As the trees swayed, each shrouded in shadows
Of glimmering ochres and greys.

But the sun rose up higher through Heaven,
And splashes of sunlight appeared
Through the leaflets of trees overlapping,
As Morning through rosy skies peered.

And amidst shady groves I stood, dappled
With silhouettes cast from above,
While the dewdrops hung round me like crystals,
As soft as the tears from a dove,

Each inverting and changing its image,
Distorting the forest and trees.
And the Voice of the Winds called me forwards,
Borne swiftly on Morning's light breeze.

And I followed, to see through the clearing,
The forest pool, glassy and bright;
Its calm surface in clear violescence
Reflecting the dawn's filtered light.

Swirling ripples raced madly in circles,
Increasing, till, skimming from view,
More appeared from the central gyration,
Each polychromatic in hue.

And I yearned for the pool to caress me,
As I on the bankside stood long.
And the Voice of the Winds called me onwards
In lyrical segments of song.

So I entered, and felt the pool's wonder
Embrace me in eager repose.
And I gazed through its glistening beauty,
As o'er me its silhouette rose.

Here I stood 'midst its clear undulations,
And Weight left my beckoning soul.
Now the world lay below me in silence –
A solitary, orbiting bowl.

And I stood in this limitless limbo,
Where all was a daydream sublime,
And the Voice of the Winds called me upwards,
To Doorways of Heaven, and Time.

I have always harboured a somewhat Quixotic captivation for windmills, and this following poem was inspired by the very eyecatching cover of a 1970s record album that featured a spectacular, multicoloured image of a windmill created by time-lapse photography, in which its arms seemed to be turning not merely through the air but also through space and even through time itself.

The Windmill

Like an astral wheel of Heaven
Sweeping silently through Space,
Never ceasing, never easing
In its convoluted pace,

Like an outward-coiling spiral
As its spool spins ever on
Through the webs of Space forever
Till its silhouette has gone,

Past the stars all draped in wonder
As its whirling arms sweep down
Through the solitudes of darkness
In the evening's velvet gown.

Still its shadow keeps on turning
Past the zenith of the skies,
For the windmill's winding pivot
Is where Time most surely lies,

E'er gyrating on its axis
Like a pendulum in Space,
As through depthless pools and chasms
Its unwinding fingers trace –

Like a clock revolving slowly,
Lacking rhythm, lacking rhyme,
Just rotating through the heavens
As the centre-stone of Time.

Imagine a multicoloured flight of winged Faerie folk, flitting swiftly from their hidden world through the realms of dreams to greet the dawning day, then on through forgotten lands of shadow until night appears, whereupon they return at last to their own secret world. That's what I did – and this poem was the result.

Worlds of Faerie

Small songbirds sing and bluebells ring,
And Faerie folk fly through the sky.
Red, blue, and green, yet never seen,
For on swift wings they softly fly.
Past rainbow arcs, like shining larks
They flit through unseen Faerie lands,
Through clouds of blue with violet hue,
To silent seas with silver sands.

Here, waves of dreams flow on in streams
To sleepy shores where moonlight shines.
Then on they fly through silken sky,
To elvish realms where shadows line
Each dawning day, as sunlit fays
Draw golden trains across the skies.
Still on they speed, where sunlight leads
To lands forgotten, draped in sighs
Of clouded grey, which overlay
These worlds with hazy mists of gloom.
Where nothing's real, as phantoms steal
Across their lands and on to doom.

But fairies turn where sunlight burns
Down warm upon the countryside.
Then Night draws near, so on they steer
To fairy groves, in which they glide,
Away from eyes that seek to pry
Into the secrets of their world,
Which stays apart from human hearts
Until, to Time, is all unfurled.

PART 3:
A SENSE OF MYSTERY

Even as a child, the ordinary world was never enough for me – I was always irresistibly attracted to everything that was extraordinary, mysterious, fabulous, unexpected (making my interest in cryptozoology, for instance, an inevitability). Consequently, it should come as no surprise to discover that such themes have inspired many of my poems too, as revealed in the following selection.

> If, when hearing that I have been stilled at last, they stand at the door,
> Watching the full-starred heavens that winter sees,
> Will this thought rise on those who will meet my face no more,
> "He was one who had an eye for such mysteries"?

Thomas Hardy – 'Afterwards'

> Dark, black giant butterflies
> kill the radiance of the sun.
> And earthwards from the sky
> the monsters invisible,
> with heavy pinions, sink
> down upon the hearts of men.

Albert Giraud – 'Night', in *Pierrot Lunaire*

When the evening wind blusters lustily through the willows, are they merely being blown from side to side in passive defeat, or could it be that they are dancing in moonlit wistfulness, unseen by the sleeping eyes of mankind as they perform their graceful ballet and murmur sad melodies beneath a bright panoply of stars?

Ballet of the Willows

Softly the moon glides in cloud-cushioned orbit
Far through the star-sequined shades of the skies,
Wafting through Space like a shimmering teardrop
Silently falling from Night's velvet eyes.
And as the stars blink through lavender curtains,
Twinkling their heavenly lanterns of light,
Nightingale rhapsodies sail through the woodlands,
Sweet dulcet music to serenade Night,

Drifting 'cross lakesides where willows sway gently –
Boughs kissed by starlight as downwards they bend,
Arching, as crescents of silver-shot rainbows
Dance through their branches, while moon shaftlets wend
Downwards to die in the willows' reflection –
Trapped like a thought in the mirrors of Space –
Fading from sight as the willows' soft murmurs
Ripple and rise o'er the lake's silver face,

Whispering gently in long chords of sadness
Dreams from the very beginning of time,
Singing in voices each soft yet unending,
Hauntingly wistful yet strangely sublime,
Swaying in dance as the swift evening breezes
Spiral and curl through their emerald leaves,
Combing them gently with cool twilit fingers,
Stroking each softly as round them they weave,

Silently laughing like souls of the evening,
Mournfully sighing like ghosts of the dawn,
Leaving at last as the sun rises slowly,
Borne on the wings of the first breath of morn.
And as the sun paints its glorious murals
Far 'cross the heavens in burnishing hue,
Silent and still are the tall golden willows,
Each weeping diamonds of glittering dew.

Yet, far above them, through vast cloudy strata,
Still their soft voices soar upwards and on.
E'er will they sing in the vales of the future,
E'en when the whispering willows have gone,
E'en when their lakeside reflection has faded –
Melting like gold 'neath the sun's crimson face –
Ne'er more to snare their ethereal beauty,
Lost like a dream in the cobwebs of Space.

Fantasy horses – such as unicorns, flying horses, and star steeds – have always held a particular fascination for me, as will be revealed in this section. So here is the first of several variations upon this exotic equine theme – the thunder horse, which features in the traditional legends of North America's Sioux tribe. Interestingly, during the 19th Century the Sioux showed various scientists some huge bones said to be from thunder horses, and when these were examined they were found to be the fossilised remains of a hitherto-undescribed form of gigantic prehistoric mammal distantly related to rhinoceroses, which scientists duly christened Brontotherium *– the thunder beast.*

Behold the Thunder Horse

Dark lie the skies, as an ebony ocean
Rippling with cloudlets of surf-showered foam,
Lashed by the whipcords of storm-harnessed lightning,
Raking the heavens with bright fiery combs,

Savagely striking like flame-spitting cobras
Flicking their tongues through the vapours of Night,
Streaking through Space like a phalanx of dragons –
Melting the candlewax stars in their flight.

And as the skies part their dark, scorching curtains
Lit by the flickering shadows of fire,
Out from the flames rears a black steed of thunder,
Phoenix-wise born from a burnishing pyre –

Eyes blazing fiercely like crimson infernos,
Flashing like meteors bolting through Space,
Flames roaring loudly through dark velvet nostrils,
Framing with fire his illustrious face –

Streaming to Earth like a star cast from Heaven,
Wingtips alight with vermillion plumes,
Tail tossing high, now a flickering candle
Burning a trail through the smouldering gloom.

And as he lands on a grey, brooding mountain,
Mane ruffling far like a meadow of fire,
Thunder is borne from his deafening hoof-beats,
Echoing far like a vast booming choir.

Clashing in Space, these celestial cymbals
Loudly resound through the battle-torn skies,
Shredded and shattered by arrows of lightning
Shooting like flames from the thunder gods' eyes –

Gazing to Earth as their mighty steed races
Far 'cross the mountains in glorious flight,
Hooves ringing far, as the star on his forehead
Slashes the heavens with sabres of light.

Onward he surges, through hillside and valley,
Singeing the treetops with each fiery roar,
Vomiting flames like a spurting volcano
Booming with menace from skyline to shore.

Yet as he glows like a lava-lit furnace
Far through the sequin-sewn shades of the night,
Evening flits softly from purple-hued heavens,
Bidding farewell as she passes from sight,

Leaving the skies now as slumbering Morning
Shakes off her rose-petal blankets of sleep,
Soon to ascend through the clouds, soft and fleecy –
Frolicking gaily like clusters of sheep –

Bearing the sun like a glistening globule
Dripping its molten aurorae through Space,
Hanging it deftly from Heaven's bright archway,
Lighting in splendour her shimmering face.

And as she smiles in the sun's golden mirror,
Thunderclouds wilt, sinking downwards to die,
Blown from the heavens by Morning's gay laughter,
Nothing remains but a soft lonely sigh.

Now, far below, like an ebony shadow,
Rising on pinions emblazoned with fire,
Swiftly their stallion soars through the heavens,
Upwards once more to his ultimate pyre,

Swiftly approaching the sun's bright corona –
Hung like a burnishing nimbus in Space –
Nearer and nearer, till wingtip and halo
Melt into one 'midst the heaven's warm face.

Gone is the steed of the storm cloud and thunder –
Far past the dawn's bright eruption of light –
Lost in the radiant sun's incandescence
Borne through the clouds in its luminous flight.

Yet if the thunder gods e'er should roar loudly
Far through the heavens of some future night,
Then would he rise in a great conflagration,
Streaming on pinions of flame-feathered light,

Scorching through Space like a blazing colossus,
Tail curving high like a smouldering lyre,
Spraying with flames this caliginous shadow –
Borne into life by the spirit of fire.

When I wrote this poem during the 1970s, the threat of nuclear devastation was uppermost in many people's minds, with the bombing of Hiroshima and Nagasaki a mere three decades earlier. Another three decades have now passed, and, with them, I pray, the danger that these verses' dread scenario might one day come to pass.

The Bomb

Like an incandescent mushroom
Rising slowly through the skies,
As its image heaves and billows
In a shadowed cloak of sighs.

Thus it grows, a mournful spectre
From a silent world of gloom,
As it surges up, still watching
O'er a dead, forgotten tomb.

Clouds of darkness hang, suspended
From its parapet of death.
All have felt the bitter lustre
Of its all-consuming breath.

And below, a final mutant
Writhes in silence, pale and wan,
For his form is undistinguished,
Yet this creature once was Man –

At the feet of his creation,
Now released to enter Space,
Laughing inwardly in silence
As its dark, despairing face

Gazes down to watch its maker,
Left to shrink in fear and cry
'Neath a choking veil of vapour
'Ere he crawls away to die.

Now the shadow rises upwards,
For its work has been fulfilled.
Just like all, it had a purpose
That the Shining One had willed.

Radiation's shrouded Doorway
Had been opened to the world.
If Man could have only known that
Death himself had been unfurled.

Surrounded by her minions of many kinds, the Fairy Queen slumbers peacefully through the starlit wonder of a summer's night, guarded from prying eyes, and lulled by the nightingale's lilting song...

Fairy Lullaby

Speak not near our Fairy Queen, you spotted snakes and warty toads;
Fly not near our Fairy Queen, you wingèd bats of fields and roads.
Bring her peace this summer night, and let sweet scent fill air and space,
Charming Sleep to bring her slumber as the moon shines o'er her face.

Philomel, with sweet enchantment, sing to her your song of Night,
While the moon moves through the heavens in its pale, bewitching flight,
Like a pool of dreams and lullabies whose notes drift down to Earth,
Borne on wings of silver moonlight that to Mystery gave birth.

Spiders small, with spots of stardust twinkling softly in the night,
Draw not near our Fairy Queen as on your webs you race in flight;
Shining beetles, black and armoured, scuttle far from fairy eyes,
Or King Oberon's great chariot you'll draw through evening skies.

Till the rosy dawn arises from the snowy clouds of Sleep,
May you rest in worlds beyond us, in a slumber warm and deep.
And when Morning has appeared, then may you wake and fly away,
In your carriage drawn by butterflies, to greet the newborn day.

One of the most exquisite examples of cinematic animation that I have ever seen is contained within the 'Pastoral Symphony' segment of Walt Disney's animated masterpiece 'Fantasia', and features a phalanx of flying horses spiralling downwards from the sky to settle gracefully upon the surface of a sparkling blue lake. The following poem is my word-picture homage to that breathtakingly beautiful scene.

Flying Horse Fantasia

From the heavens' rainbowed archways
To the clear blue lake below
Soars a flock of flying horses,
Down and down, where rivers flow
Round the willows and the fountains,
Past the sparkling waterfalls,
To the mountains and the valleys,
Where lone Echo softly calls.

Down and down they swoop in glory,
Flowing manes and silver tails,
Through the lilac clouds of Summer,
Over meadowlands and vales.
Round they circle, wheeling swiftly
In a graceful sweeping flight,
As the sky pours forth its tribute
In a shower of golden light.

Down they glide towards the water
As their wondrous wings surge round.
Then alighting on the surface,
They fold back without a sound,
As these equine swans of Summer
Drift across the azure lake,
Heads held high in noble splendour,
Pinions trailing in their wake.

Blossom swirls upon the waters
Like a host of golden charms,
While the air is filled with singing,
And the sound of murmured psalms.
Then the wingèd colts neigh loudly
As their graceful parents glide
Far across the lustrous waters
To the lake's far-distant side.

Both as regal as the sunset,
One as snowy as a dove,
And the other, black as Midnight,
Each with eyes so full of love,
As they call in dulcet voices
To their boisterous colts behind,
Shining blue, and pink, and lemon,
Flowing manes all intertwined.

And as Morning's sunlight shimmers
On the waters' mirror bright,
It reflects five flying horses
Soaring slowly out of sight,
Past the golden drifts of sunbeams,
And the shadows of the morn,
To idyllic lands beyond them
In a pastel-shaded dawn.

When I was younger, my grandmother, Mrs Gertrude Timmins, told me of how, one evening many years earlier, she and other members of her family had stood in her bedroom watching three brightly-coloured UFOs circling back and forth for quite a while in the skies above their home in the town of Wednesbury, in the West Midlands, England, before eventually flying away, never to return. Not having seen a UFO, I had to content myself by imagining how it might be if I ever did do so.

The Flying Saucer

Through the night-time's spangled valleys
My enquiring eyes raced far,
Still enchanted by the beauty
Of each twinkling evening star,

When a hazy gleam surged outwards
From a chasm deep in Space.
And its eldritch light grew brighter,
Darting swiftly 'cross my face –

Like a stream of glowing fingers
Chasing softly through my hair
In a multicoloured spectrum
'Mid the evening's breathless air.

Then the gleam became a halo
Spinning slowly through the sky,
As the moon cast ghostly shadows,
Sinking ever down to die.

Soon a shape became apparent
In this strange, unearthly glow.
Now a humming sphere, it circled,
As its light began to grow,

In a luminous suffusion,
Till, when slowly gliding by,
I could feel its eerie presence
Probing deeply through my eyes.

And I sensed at once that, there, some
Strange intelligence looked down,
One that watched with eyes unblinking
O'er the sombre, sleeping town.

Then the phosphorescent globule
Glided silently away,
In a cosmic orb of aura
Through the heavens draped in grey,

Till its weird, fluorescent image
Faded slowly from my sight.
And my eyes were left to wander
Through the shadows of the night.

But that alien aurora
Still cast shivers o'er my face,
As I gazed in spellbound wonder
Through the catacombs of Space,

In the fear that one dark night it
Will return amid the gloom,
Like a strange, unearthly phantom
From the abysses of Doom.

Haunted houses are normally ten a penny, nothing special – but this poem's ghost-associated cottage is very special, very different, as you will discover…

The Haunted Cottage

Deep in a green woodland vale wrapped in sunbeams
Stands a small cottage, alone and afar;
Windows still shining, transparent and lucent,
Each pane alight like a shimmering star.

Over the walls clings a shroud of green ivy,
Crisp arrowed leaves shot with yellowing veins;
Emerald spear-heads outsplayed in the sunlight,
Beaming and gleaming from warm noontide rain.

Briars glisten softly with wet, fragrant roses,
Sending forth beauty in sweet-scented bliss;
Each one half-opened as if still in slumber,
Waiting for Summer's awakening kiss.

Swallows skim swiftly from chimney to gable,
Mazarine star-bolts with waistcoats of flame;
Aerial gymnasts each vaulting o'er cloudlets,
Chasing and racing in sky-diving games.

Spiders spin curtains of gossamer fabric,
Hanging serenely from windows and walls;
Light as the soft gauzy drapings of Faerie,
Murals suspended in Oberon's halls.

Blossom drifts gently down over the cottage,
Apple and cherry cast far from above;
Fragile and fragrant it sails on the zephyr,
Borne on the wingtips of Nature's warm love.

So it seems strange that this cottage is haunted –
For, if we enter its small shaded rooms,
Phantoms ne'er loom forth to frighten or mutter,
Nothing appears from the shadows and gloom.

But if we let this small cottage's image
Out of our sight for a moment or less,
When we look back, we will search for it vainly –
For it has gone, we will have to confess.

Although no spectres appear in its bedrooms,
There is a phantom of which it can boast.
And its strange secret it holds to this day – for
This lonely cottage itself is the ghost.

This wouldn't be a book of mine if cryptozoology didn't rear its head in it somewhere! So here, for mystery beast lovers everywhere, is a little snippet of crypto-history – the very first piece of writing that I ever penned (over 30 years ago!) in relation to the most famous cryptid of all. Nessie, this one's for you!

The Loch Ness Monster

Through swirling mists of early morn,
Across the loch's dull light,
A dark shape moves with hidden power,
Then disappears from sight
Beneath Loch Ness's murky cloak
Of water black and cold.
What lives in this vast underworld,
In Ness's misty fold?

What creature thrives below the waves,
Beneath the surface grim?
What beast appears in photographs –
Obscure, opaque, and dim?
What creature gave the myths and tales
From bygone days new fame?
Of water horses, fierce, malign,
Which from the waters came,
To strike the hearts of every man
With terror of their forms.
The kelpies – dark, malignant ghosts,
And harbingers of storms.

So what gave all these legends life –
A creature huge in size,
With tiny horns and rhomboid limbs,
And glowing, deathless eyes?
A relic from the ancient past,
Disturbed by modern worlds?
It will be long, indeed, before
This secret is unfurled.

Hidden deep within the shadowed lands of Faerie is the garden of their king, Oberon – a setting of magical delight, where shy unicorns roam in freedom, bright flowers sing with dulcet voices, and Oberon's entrancing queen, Mab, reposes in sunlit splendour. Let us step inside this enchanted place for a moment, and see what we shall see...

Oberon's Garden

Sing, yellow linnet, of Oberon's garden –
Mystical, wonderful, strange to behold,
Hidden away in the deep realms of Faerie,
Dappled in shadows of green and of gold.

Here singing flowers trill their soft lilting music,
Violets, red roses, and other fair blooms,
Borne from all seasons to serenade softly
Oberon, resting in gossamer rooms.

And through these gardens enchanted and lovely
Bright wingèd steeds flit from rainbows to streams.
Timid and shy, here the unicorns frolic,
Misty and distant as overnight dreams.

Pixies race swiftly on glittering beetles,
Harnessed with gossamer, saddled with leaves,
Past tinkling fountains and waterfalls tumbling,
Through groves and woodlands each chariot weaves.

Mab lies serenely in deep beds of sunshine,
Graceful and pale as the bright morning star,
Strange fairy beauty, enchanting and mystic,
Born in a land that lies hidden afar.

Now, as the evening draws o'er this strange setting,
Stars twinkle softly like lanterns of Night,
And when we look back at Oberon's garden,
We shall find that it has vanished from sight.

It has slipped back to the kingdom it came from,
Back to the fairyland realms of the past,
For in our world nothing lives on forever –
Not even fairies forever may last.

Scientists tell us that seafarers' stories of mermaids were really based upon sightings of seals, manatees, and other homely-looking marine mammals – a far cry, indeed, if true, from the bewitchingly beautiful mermaid of legend, as encountered in the following poem.

Perchance a Mermaid?

Raised through the laughter of shimmering oceans
Rests a lone pinnacle, gloomy and grey,
Sombre in form 'gainst a bright turquoise surface,
Silently cursing the coming of Day.

But, as the spirals of ripple and wavelet
Gently embellish this courtier of Night,
High on its peak – as the dawn now exposes,
Bathing her softly in fountains of light –

Slumbers a mermaid 'neath blankets of bubbles
Cast from the surface in shining array.
And as she wakens, they flit from her bedside,
Kissing her fondly like transient fays.

Slowly she rises, and smiles at the sunlight,
Dancing in sprays of bright saffron and gold.
And as she rests there, her glittering fishtail
Swirls in the depths of the sea's liquid folds,

Spinning each wave like a radiant vortex,
Twirling through chateaux of coral and shells,
Chasing a seahorse with fluted adornments
Gaily through undersea valleys and dells.

And as the ocean caresses her gently,
Zephyrs flit long through her shimmering hair,
Stroking it softly with murmuring fingers,
Kissing each rivulet, golden and fair,

Beaming like waterfalls gleaming and lucent,
Gaily cascading in glistening light,
As she combs slowly through each ruffling ringlet,
Holding a murex shell pearly and white,

Calmly reposing 'neath heavens of glory
Caught in the ocean's reflection of blue,
While, as its mirror refracts their resplendence,
Rays filter downwards in spectrum-split hues

Each to disperse through the sea's silent darkness,
Lighting its kingdom with shadows of green,
Piercing its dreaming with malachite shaftlets,
Darting with arrows of aquamarine.

And as the morn flushes brightly in Heaven,
Clouds drift so slowly by, moving e'er on.
Then, as the sun gazes down on the mermaid,
Swiftly she glides through the waves, and is gone –

Drawn through the sea as its echoing whispers
Sail on the breeze, gusting out and away,
Far to horizons where shores gently slumber,
Lit by the reincarnation of Day.

The inspiration for this poem came from Maurice Maeterlinck's classic play, The Blue Bird, *a delightful fantasy work first produced in 1908 that seems nowadays to have become almost forgotten, yet which is filled with wonderfully evocative scenes and imaginative personifications.*

The Pool of Dreams

'Midst the cerulean heavens
Lies the fabled Pool of Dreams,
Veiled in rosy mists of Slumber
Casting tender lilac beams
Through its cyanescent waters
To its darkened depths of blue,
Each transforming purple ripples
Into iridescent hues
Racing swiftly o'er its surface
Like a phalanx borne from Light,
Flitting rainbows glinting brightly
'Ere they disappear from sight.

For the dreams of sleeping mankind
Lie within this glossy pool,
Which releases them like phantoms
To emerge through evenings cool
In the drowsing worlds of mortals –
Empty shadows of the mind,
Which with rapturous enchantment
Mortals' conscious spirits bind,
Till the morning's pale suffusion
Rises softly through the sky,
Then away through twilit heavens
To the Pool of Dreams they fly.

And within its silken waters
Lies each tiny unborn child,
Sleeping long in drowsy silence,
As the Pool's reflection mild
Shines upon these infant dreamers,
Till their mothers softly pray,
Then they wake from golden slumber,
And are borne on sunlit rays
Down to Earth, where every mother
Will, her newborn babes, embrace,
As their tiny eyes then open
And behold their mother's face.

Yet among the Pool's clear waters
Lies a dead child, for he lay
So entranced within his slumber
That he dreamt his life away.
But the angels take him softly
On their snowy wings of Peace,
For from Life's harsh world beneath them
They have given him release.
Now between the clouds of violet
Like a cherub winged he flies,
To the Glory that is Heaven,
'Midst the splendour of the skies.

As a teenager at school, I was impressed enough by a scraperboard picture of a star steed produced by a friend to purchase it from him for the princely sum of £5, and also to write the following poem in homage to the celestial stallion that it portrays. Over 30 years later, that picture can be seen on this book's front cover.

The Star Horse

Into the sea's erupting foam,
Concealed by Evening's shades,
A star descends from Heaven's vale
'Ere Twilight's beauty fades.

And from the sapphire turbulence
A starry beam is borne –
A hazy mist of twinkling light,
A strange, auroral dawn.

And soon an outline bright appears
Within this gleaming force –
A silhouette in silver, of
A shining, starlit horse,

Emerging from the bubbling depths
With sparkling, ruffling mane,
And eyes that dart like icy stars
From Evening's dappled train.

His body glints with rippling light
As clear as starfire rays –
A flowing spirit borne through Space
To islands far away,

To race across the mauve lagoons
'Neath Heaven's silent gaze.
And though the moon sends clouded light,
She knows he ne'er long stays.

For soon the sky recalls this steed
Of starry, dreaming Space.
And so he leaves on sparkling hooves
Past Earth's immortal face.

From Space into Eternity
He goes where none have flown,
A spirit wild with nature mild,
A ghost fore'er alone

Amongst a vast Infinity
That stretches ever on,
A phantom flitting long till Dawn
Arrives to see him gone.

But Evening watches o'er this steed
From far-off realms sublime,
And still the fourth dimension waits
For him – the soul of Time.

No-one who has visited Stonehenge, as I first did a decade or so ago, can fail to be impressed by its aloof, stark grandeur, embodying a remote agelessness that effortlessly transcends the tedious minutiae of our modern-day world – hearkening back instead to an unimaginably distant time, yet quite conceivably lingering on, unblemished, long after we have vanished elsewhere, leaving behind a dead, desecrated planet to this ancient monument's silent, eternal vigil.

Stonehenge

Like a ring of empty windows
'Neath the mirrors of the sky,
Draped in silhouettes of Silence
As the evening's phantoms die

In the hush of newborn Morning
From the clouds each hung in sleep,
While the moon sinks down to slumber
And the stars so softly weep.

But these pinnacles of Shadow
Notice not those tears of dew,
Theirs is Past alone – not Present –
From which long ago they grew

Changing ne'er, as if forgotten
By the sentinels of Time,
While the winds breathe murmured echoes
Like a stream of ghostly chimes

Through their empty arching doorways
To the meadows of the Past,
For their pagan ring of darkness
Seems forever more to last,

Like a cold, unending nimbus
Where the sun has never shone.
And their ancient chill still lingers
As their dismal forms stretch on

In a mesmerising circle,
Like a world removed from all,
While the years flit by, pale shadows
'Neath their stony, rugged walls.

They have watched the silver starships
Glide away through silent Space,
Growing fainter every moment
Till they passed beyond their face.

And behind, a dying planet
Drew its last polluted breath
'Neath a shroud of radiation
'Ere it sank away to death.

Yet these sombre tombs of Silence
Lingered still though all had gone,
Penetrating through the darkness
As their forms stretched ever on.

They – alone – who could not crumble;
They – alone – who could not die;
Still persisting, silhouetted
'Gainst a vacant, empty sky.

What would happen, I wonder, if, tired of being slain by knights errant, the ancient dragons of evil decided to adopt new guises in order to survive and continue spreading their malign influence within the modern world of mankind?

Transforming the Dragon

Are you there, o monstrous dragon,
Coal-black scales like pools of Night?
Are your hellfire eyes still burning,
Flaming orbs of scarlet light?

Do your spiralled horns still glitter
On your brow like evil towers?
And your heart of bitter longing,
Does it bloom like fiery flowers?

Old you are, yet ever-changing,
No more gusts of toxic breath,
Spurts of fire through roaring nostrils,
Beating wings, or gaze of death.

Smitten by St George's valour,
Risen now to strike anew,
Born again in new disguises,
More deceptive now, as through

All the lands you steal unnoticed,
No more talons, scales, or flame.
Now you dress in human garments,
Yet your soul remains the same –

Tempting human minds to vanquish
All the love they know is true,
In the guise of friends or kinsfolk,
Those that they feel closest to.

So beware of all such dragons,
Different though they may have grown.
They alone Death dare not call on,
Lest they turn e'en him to stone.

The concept of Quetzalcoatl – an Aztec serpent god adorned with feathers rather than scales, and gifted with the ability to soar majestically through the heavens without needing wings – is one that has long fascinated me, so it was inevitable that sooner or later I would attempt to capture the wonder of this spectacular reptilian deity in verse.

A Tribute to Quetzalcoatl

Green feathered serpent like Heaven's liana,
Plumes of bright malachite, jasper, and jade,
Furled in rich flourishes, dazzling in glory,
Verdurous rays borne on emerald blades.

And, as you gleam in your jewel-clustered temple,
Coils gliding over your tributes of gold,
Ruby eyes glow with the flames of the cosmos,
Deadly yet passionate, blazing but cold.

Now, as your lightning-forked tongue flickers brightly,
Sibilant breath hissing softly and long,
Bowing before you in rapt veneration
Kneel your disciples in reverent throngs.

Yet, do you laugh at these weak, puny mortals,
Scuttling like ants in the fire of your gaze,
Shielding their eyes in the depths of your shadow –
Turquoise and terrible, willing their praise?

Quetzalcoatl – ophidian idol,
Soaring through Space like a radiant stream.
Aztec divinity, ageless, eternal –
Incarnate god, or a deified dream?

Over the years, I've written a number of short compositions, rhyming and non-rhyming, to serve mostly as chapter openers for a variety of different publications (and sometimes even using a pseudonym), but which, I feel, deserve the opportunity to stand alone in their own right as poetry. Here is a brief, representative selection.

The Unicorn

A shaft of bright golden sunbeams broke through the leafy canopy of the forest, illuminating a clearing deep within its verdant, secluded heart - and also illuminating a wondrous creature, standing sedately like a living statue hewn from shimmering starlight.

It resembled an elegant snowy-hued horse, but its noble brow bore a single, central horn - long and finely spiralled, upon which the sunbeams joyfully danced.

Here was the forest guardian, the very spirit of nature incarnate - for this was that most rare and fabulous of animals, the unicorn.

Suddenly, however, the distant sound of a hunting horn pierced the stillness of this magical scene.

Instantly alert, the unicorn raised its head, momentarily betraying flickers of alarm, and of sadness too, within its shining eyes.

Then, as softly as the echo of a single heartbeat, it was gone, lost to human sight and knowledge within its woodland sanctuary.

Dragons

Dragons!

Fire-belching damsel devourers mortally skewered upon a valiant knight's lance, or ethereal serpentine deities wafting languorously through the skies in celestial tranquillity.

Vermiform monsters with coils of steel, or winged wonders with jewel-encrusted scales.

Bat-winged nightmares that terrorise and desecrate with volcanic gullets of flame, or polychromatic dream beasts soaring heavenward upon iridescent plumes of crystalline glory.

Personifications of malevolence or beneficence, paganism or purity, death and devastation, life and fertility, good or evil.

All of these varied, contradictory concepts are embodied and embedded within that single magical word!

Tattoos

Our tattoos are the stained-glass windows of our soul,
Which illuminate and animate our drab external shell
With the dreams, fantasies, and desires
Of our transient mortal existence
Within the mundane, earthbound realm of reality.

Mirabilis

Let not the dream pervade these living hours,
Lest the winged cats of nightmare stalk once more
The haunted spires of distant memory,
Their pinions raised, alert and poised
To deny the conscious dawn.

The Panther

Velveteen silhouette, silent and sinister;
Satin-furred midnight on ebony paws.
Eyes hewn from emeralds, seeking a sacrifice;
Death to deliver with ivory claws.

PART 4:
LOOKING FORWARD, LOOKING BACK

It was the British playwright Arthur Wing Pinero who wrote: "I believe the future is only the past again, entered through another gate", and all of the poems in this section were inspired by fond memories of bygone times, dreams of what may be still to come, and the subtle but complex interplay of past, present, and future that imperceptibly encompasses our world.

I remember, I remember,
The house where I was born,
The little window where the sun
Came peeping in at morn;
He never came a wink too soon,
Nor brought too long a day,
But now, I often wish the night
Had borne my breath away…

I remember, I remember,
The fir trees dark and high;
I used to think their slender tops
Were close against the sky:
It was a childish ignorance,
But now 'tis little joy
To know I'm farther off from Heav'n
Than when I was a boy.

Thomas Hood – 'I Remember, I Remember'

Come to the Land of Youth: the trees grown heavy there
Drop on the purple wave the starry fruit they bear.
Drink: the immortal waters quench the spirit's longing.
Art thou not now, bright one, all sorrows past, in elation,
Made young with joy, grown brother-hearted with the vast,
Whither thy spirit wending flits the dim stars past
Unto the Light of Lights in burning adoration.

George William Russell – 'A Call of the Sidhe'

Strange as it may sound, this is one poem that quite literally wrote itself. There was no planning, no previous thought involved – I simply sat down one day with a blank sheet of paper and pen, the words came unbidden into my head, and I wrote them down, acting as little more than a thoroughfare along which the verses coursed, fully-formed, from my mind and onto the paper. If only all poetry were as easy to write!

Borne Into Tomorrow

The webs of Night draw back their gowns
As rosy clouds of Morning
Pass softly through the waking sky,
While still the sun lies yawning
Beneath a drape of starry sleep
From which the dreams of Evening peep.

But mine are dreams from far beyond,
Sent ever by the future,
Like golden keys to shrouded doors
Of Nature's hidden sutures.
For these, my life must make its ways
Through shadow worlds and lightless days.

Alone I stand – my world has gone –
The past was mine, not present.
Now shades of Death lie all around.
As I – a humble peasant –
Move slowly through and ever on,
Until my dreams at last are done.

These worlds are strange, unknown to me,
For these I have no feeling.
And only stars may see my grief
From Heaven's spangled ceiling,
As on I pass through sombre dawns
While e'er for Light my spirit mourns.

But I must bear my silent doom
In alien surroundings,
And suffer as the world demands
Of me – a lonely foundling,
With dreams for which my spirit lives,
For which my life I freely give.

And so, though oft my chosen way
Is dismal and despairing,
I must prevail through dark terrains
Within this world uncaring,
Through deathly vales where shadows loom,
Before my dreams can light their gloom.

Yet this is but a twilit zone
Of deep, forbidding sorrow,
Which all must e'er endure if they
Are borne into Tomorrow,
Until their dreams are each fulfilled,
As Destiny and Fate have willed.

But when at last my pathways end,
When dreams are dreams no longer,
My world will call, with songs of Peace,
My spirit – free and stronger.
And I shall go, and this will seem
To be at most a bitter dream.

Some of the happiest days of my childhood were spent strolling through the fields and forests near my home. Today, many of those beautiful retreats are gone, paved over and lost beneath the ever-encroaching shadow of urban settlement, but I see them still in my mind's eye, and there is no doubt that part of my essence lingers on in those green and pleasant lands of my youth.

A Call From My Past

Back to the countryside's
Still morning air,
Where grass softly sways, for
My heart remains there.

Small singing birds perching
On leaf-covered trees,
The sun shining down on
Small yellow-striped bees

That gather sweet nectar
From every wild flower.
Magnificent Nature,
For this is her hour.

The field-mice in cornfields,
The swans on the lakes –
All Nature's perfections,
Not man-made mistakes.

And as I gaze fondly
On all that I see,
A child's voice sounds softly,
It's calling to me –

The voice of my childhood,
The laugh of a child
Who listened, and followed,
The call of the wild.

The poignant image of the clown who secretly weeps beneath his painted-on smile, whose staged laughter conceals his real tears, is both powerful and prolific, having appeared in countless forms, but assuredly attaining its zenith in the Leoncavallo opera 'Pagliacci'. It was after watching a performance of this, and hearing its most famous, sorrowful aria, 'Vesti La Giubba' ('On With The Motley'), that I penned my own variation upon this tragic, universal theme.

The Clown

Here, 'midst the tinsel and stars of the circus,
Stand I, before yet another vile crowd,
Gaping and gazing in leering distortion
Long, as their laughter rings raucously loud.

But know they not of the face that lies weeping
'Neath coats of greasepaint, of white and of red.
Know they the sadness I keep trapped within me?
Know they the clear pearly tears that I've shed

Through endless buckets of cold chilling water,
Thrown at my face for the crowds' grisly glee?
Tears that run rivers down pale whitewash features,
As all the hate and the envy I see

Circles, encompassing people and kingdoms,
All glaring at me through cold eyes of stone,
Stone as the hearts of the crowd now before me.
Gone is true love, leaving me all alone,

Lost in a world knowing not the true laughter
That I produced in those days long since past.
Nothing remains in a world ever changing,
Not even laughter forever may last.

Yet still I stay, like the great Pagliaccio,
Always I've known that the show must go on.
Put on the greasepaint and bow to the cheering,
Though all the spirit of laughter has gone.

For tonight gave I my greatest performance,
Giving my all for the bellows and jeers.
Yet did they know my lugubrious laughter
Served but to cover my visage of tears?

The ending of childhood and the onward journey through the teenage years toward maturity is never an easy passage. It is a time filled and fraught with doubt, confusion, and decisions about which pathways, in which directions, to take.

Dismissing Childhood

Alone I stand, alone with Fate.
My shadow lies ahead, to wait
For me to come, perhaps too late.

My Past flits by, my Future grows;
I ask myself: "Which way to go?"
And answer still: "I do not know."

Alone I stay, and softly sigh
To watch my childhood flutter by,
Then turn away, and wonder why.

My changing world through dreams I saw,
As onward e'er my thoughts they bore,
But now my dreams are dreams no more.

And now alone with Fate I stand,
Soon to be taken by the hand
And led away to other lands.

Yet what my Future hides away
'Neath golden shades of unknown days
I cannot know, for who can say?

I only know that this must be,
Its light is not for me to see,
For this will be my Destiny.

I owe not only my lifelong love of poetry but also my own inspiration to write poetry to this poem, which was a joint effort between myself and my mother. It began life as a school assignment at a time when I had yet to make any serious attempt at writing poetry. My mother wrote the outline of it, which I then expanded, and in so doing realised how much I was enjoying creating an original poem. And the rest, as they say, is history. The narrator of the poem is me, as a youngster; Mary-Rose is my mother, Mary Shuker; and the airman represents my mother's first husband, a young RAF pilot called Harold Hooper, who died shortly after World War II ended, as a direct result of the war.

A Ghost From The Past

My friend and companion is dear Mary-Rose,
A great nature lover as everyone knows.
She travels with me over long country miles,
Through deep greening woodlands and over the stiles.

She took me one day to her favourite place,
The sun shining brightly, the wind in her face.
She suddenly looked sad, a lone tear on her nose,
And winds whispered softly of dear Mary-Rose.

She said: "My young husband, a long time ago,
Would always come here when his spirits were low.
He'll never again come to this lovely spot,
Will never again feel the sun, oh so hot."

And then she just smiled, and said: "Come on, young man,"
And into the dingle she laughed as she ran.
We're going to watch birds, and excitement soon grows;
And a young airman whispers: "Goodbye, Mary-Rose".

My very first dog was Patch, a rough-haired Jack Russell terrier, whom I loved dearly. As he grew older (he lived for twelve and half years – a good age for his breed), he became ever more relaxed, but in his younger days he took great joy in waging war with the world outside, just like all puppies everywhere. Yet with us he was a gentle, intelligent little soul, filled with love and wisdom far beyond his species.

Patch – A Four-Legged Friend

A little whiskered face enquires
If he may join me by the fire,
For oft we sit, just he and I,
And watch the red flames flicker by.

And though the night be dark and cold,
He slumbers, reaching Sleep's calm fold
Of visitors to dreamy lands,
With silver shores and silent sands.

Yet when he wakes, he sits up straight,
Or if he's sleeping, and we're late,
He growls in puppy-thunder tones
For ending dreams of juicy bones.

But then he's up, and runs outside
To see if any cat dares ride
His fence with velvet paws of steel
That, five curved silver claws, conceal.

And if there is a bird in flight
His anger makes a dreadful sight,
As gates are mauled in raging storms
Of fury from this tiny form.

But when the world is still and calm,
Then he bodes no-one any harm.
And two dark eyes gaze up at me,
So brown and warm for all to see.

Those eyes: like liquid pools of Thought,
So dark and deep, for Nature caught
The intellect of other minds,
Of his and human thoughts combined

When she designed those shining wells
Of secrets he can never tell.
For we know not his canine speech,
As we have no-one who can teach

Us his strange tongue of howls and barks,
So we are e'er left in the dark
As to his knowledge of our world,
And truths that ne'er will be unfurled.

And yet he understands our speech,
Though he had no-one who could teach
Him, so as Life just flits us by,
Who is the dumb one – he, or I?

How many of us look back at our childhood days with fond memories and not a little sadness, recalling the summers that seemed much brighter and sunnier than they are nowadays, the flowers that blossomed more profusely, and the skies that were infused with a vivid intensity of robin's-egg blue that we can scarcely even imagine today? How many of us would willingly give up all that we have achieved in adulthood to return to the blissful happiness and security of childhood and the loving arms of our family? I would, without a moment's hesitation.

Reflections of Summers Past

'Midst golden mists and shadows cast
By summer sunbeams glowing,
'Cross straits of deep blue heavens past
The oceans gently flowing,
Glides soft enchanting sun-drenched bliss –
The warmth of Summer's loving kiss.

For here a world of sunshine lies,
Where fragrant flowers are blooming;
While silhouettes of soft mauve skies
Through mirrored pools are looming,
Reborn from silent breaths of Spring,
As delicate as fairy wings.

And here I sit in languid haze,
Caressed by wafting breezes,
Or lie in cool, refreshing laze
As sunlight gently teases,
And dream in realms of mellow green
Of amber fields, and woods serene.

And drift through lands of summers past –
Unclouded worlds of wonder –
When childhood seemed fore'er to last,
And fears I tossed asunder
As I through Nature's realms would choose
My outer shell to shed and lose.

And then, unheeded, passed I long
The hours in lone seclusion,
In worlds that more to me belong
Than modern-day illusions –
The work of Man's despairing toils,
Ensnared by Greed's unending coils.

For oft I yearn to set my gaze
Beyond the heavens' ending,
And live again those bygone days
In which my mind is wending.
One day, perhaps, my soul will fly,
And find my world beyond the sky.

I have always loved the words of William Barnes's lyrical poem 'Linden Lea', as set to music by Ralph Vaughan Williams. Listening to its evocative strains one day, and utilising the same verse form and metrical pattern per line, I composed the following poem, drawing upon the happy memories of many childhood walks of mine through the woodlands just a Sunday afternoon's drive away from home.

Remembering the Woodlands

Deep in the woodlands, sunlight filters
Through the golden leaves and flowers.
And boughs curve softly, crowned with blossom,
O'er green ferns and shadowed bowers.
Small warblers lilt in dulcet song,
As celandines in bouquets throng,
Through dappled glades and sunlit pathways,
Past blue streams and fountains clear.

Sun-shadows mottle gnarled trees arching
O'er the leafy ground of gold.
And tiny daisies wake up slowly
As their petals pink unfold.
Here snowy clouds float through the sky,
While turquoise swallows circle by,
As morningtime transforms to noontide.
Now the afternoon is here.

Though days like these soon fade and vanish
In the misty realms of Space,
With only fragments of their wonder
Passing o'er my silent face,
Yet still I live in those fair days,
In Summer's warm and blissful haze.
And as I sit, a dewdrop glistens –
Is it dew, or one lone tear?

The Robin in this poem was not a bird, but instead an elderly Scottish terrier owned by one of my grandmother's neighbours. Despite his advancing years, he always raced boisterously to greet me whenever I passed by his house, wagging his long tail wildly, and would then peer earnestly into my face with his dark expressive eyes. Sadly, Robin passed away many years ago, but for me he will always live on in this poem that I wrote as a celebration of his being.

Robin

A black-furred face peers out of doors,
Soon followed by four inky paws,
Which plod beneath his robust form
As two dark eyes, so soft and warm,

Gaze up into my smiling face,
And in them lies, perhaps, a trace
Of many long and happy years,
Recaptured still like newborn tears

By cloudy eyes windswept by Time.
Yet Time claims not those years sublime,
Remaining here within these eyes,
Which laugh in silence at the skies,

Then turn again to watch my face,
Like darkened pools of velvet Space.
And eye meets eye for seconds few,
And ageless wisdom passes through

For instants 'ere it fades and dies
On entering my human eyes.
But for a moment I have seen
A glimpse of worlds that lie between

My human life and canine worlds
Beneath those shaggy eyebrows curled.
For in that second Age met Youth,
And Life was Hope, and Wisdom, Truth.

I wrote this poem in fondest tribute to my dear grandmother, Gertrude Timmins, who, throughout the summer each year, would spend many happy hours most days in her garden of roses, lovingly tending their showy blooms, and where as a child I too spent many equally happy hours with her. Sadly, my Nan and her garden are both long gone now, but for me they are captured forever within the kindly mirror of Mnemosyne – Memory – and for the rest of the world within my verses here.

The Rose Garden

Each sunny Summer afternoon
Amongst her roses royal
A widow old as Time itself
Laboriously would toil.

Her roses grew like ruby crowns
'Midst thorns and rich green leaves.
So full of life, they seemed to speak,
Or so she would believe.

They lived for Beauty, Truth, and Life,
Like crimson furls of fire,
Whose rosy petals upwards soared,
E'er seeking to be higher.

Their scarlet hearts beat long and loud;
They only lived, it seemed,
To keep their beauty fresh and true,
Or so the lady dreamed.

For though the plants around them drooped,
They stayed unchanged through Time,
As if their very beauty gave
Them Life and Peace sublime.

And even when their own leaves died,
Their blooms rose up still higher –
Their love of Beauty burning more
Than any scorching fire.

They were their owner's greatest joy,
For them she journeyed on,
Through Life's strange world of constant change,
Her younger years far gone.

Till one fine morn she passed from sight,
Dismissing Life's dark lane,
And to her flowers her soul returned,
Ne'er leaving them again.

Perhaps one day her form we'll glimpse
Through Summer's sunlit hours –
A Queen amongst the whispers of
Her bowing court of flowers

Without a never-ending flurry of dreams stoking the restlessness of an ever-enquiring mind, the pursuit of scientific discovery could not occur – for as Friedrich Nietzsche once wrote: "You must have chaos in your heart to give birth to a dancing star."

The Scientists

Still on they seek,
For theirs are dreams,
Each thought, a life,
A shining beam
In a vast Infinity.

For theirs is Truth,
More real than ours,
More lasting.
Still on they seek through Fate's charade,
Ever.
Their dreams are Life
In future dawns,
As onward e'er
Their thoughts are borne.

Their souls live on,
For they have sown
Their timeless dreams,
Which they had grown
From a lone affinity.

Their hearts are Hope,
A burning flame
Of courage,
Still shining forth in unborn souls,
Ever.
To carry forth
In newborn brains
Their endless thoughts
In reborn veins

For Fate preserves
Their silent thoughts
In other minds,
Which Nature brought
From unseen Divinity.

Enquiring minds,
For such are these,
Of wonder,
Pursuing their unending dreams,
Ever.
For they are Time,
And ne'er will die,
Till man is cast
From Heaven's eye.

It has often been said, and it is perfectly true, that each of us enters and leaves this world alone, but it is also true that many spend much of their allotted time here in solitude too, with only silence and the stars above for company.

The Silence of Solitude

Within these dappled vales of Space
My seeking mind is found,
Amid the empty pools of Time
That softly pivot round;
For silence, long and endless, here
Is e'er the only sound.

But in this plane of nothingness
My mind can find release
From human woes and human grief,
For here, all failings cease
To be, among the silence of
This citadel of peace.

And here, my weeping tears and sighs
Can drift unseen away,
For who can know my silent doom
That lingers through each day.
For me, the loneliness I hold
No words could e'er convey.

And oft I gaze unseeing through
These misty realms of Space,
And wonder at the sadness of
The thoughts that swiftly race
Across the pale illusion of
My silent, sombre face.

Yes, I know more of loneliness
Than I could ever say,
As silently I've walked alone
Along its dismal way,
Till far ahead a Light has shone
To clarify my day.

So many times I've wondered why
I should be on my own,
While others reap their harvests in
From fields they haven't sown,
Then leave me there in silence as
I gather mine alone.

But I have long since realised
That I must strive alone
If I am e'er to find the life
I seek to claim my own,
By reaping only where I know
My silent work has sown.

So, silently, mankind may frown
To hear my wistful tones,
But e'en in death my soul must flit
Through Heaven's Door alone,
To kneel before the Glory of
God's everlasting Throne.

So let them stare, for onwards still
My thoughts must stream and pour,
If I am e'er to navigate
Beyond this present shore,
And stand amidst the silence of
The Future's open door.

In 1977, the year of the Silver Jubilee of Her Majesty the Queen, I think that it was the Daily Mirror *newspaper that held a competition, open to all unpublished poets, to write a poem celebrating this momentous occasion. In response, I penned the following poem, but in the time-honoured tradition of teenage laziness, I never got around to sending it off. Finally, after a delay of only 32 years, here it is, in print at last - so if you happen to be reading it now, Your Majesty, I apologise most sincerely for not having made it available sooner.*

A Silver Jubilee Tribute to Her Majesty Queen Elizabeth II

Far 'cross the rich verdant meadows of Britain,
Church bells chime long of the great Jubilee.
Even Britannia raises her trident
Proudly before you in praise from the sea.

Trumpets announce you and fanfares precede you,
Children smile shyly as slowly you pass.
Rose petals spiral from window and rooftop
Downwards in reverence to drift through the grass.

You are our glorious monarch and sovereign,
Bearing our might like a shimmering crown –
Set with the sadness and joys of your birthright,
Sparkling like stars in the evening's rich gown.

Yours is the fate of our kingdom, and ever
Must you alone bear our sorrows and joys.
Ne'er can the world know your innermost secrets,
Yours must be majesty, splendour, and poise.

So let us praise you this Jubilee season,
Long may you reign o'er our country serene.
Long may your years of resplendence continue –
You are our Lady, our Light, and our Queen.

This is one of many poems written by me that attempt to convey in words a detailed picture, or, more specifically in this particular instance, a mood-picture – combining the subtle changes of light and sound that attend the coming of day with the birth of new thoughts and aspirations that accompany my own awakening.

Thoughts of a Dreamer

Softly the skies part their star-dappled curtains,
Drifting from sight as the shadow of Morn
Lights up their world with her heavenly candles
Held in the warm golden hands of the dawn.

And as I watch, all alone with the morning,
Thoughts dance and ripple from dream-spangled eyes,
Racing in silence like ebony islands
Gliding through twilight 'neath faraway skies.

Onward they soar through the shimmering moonlight –
Guiding them gently through sapphire seas,
Hushed by the whispering winds of the evening,
Soothed by the murmuring songs of the trees.

Far from the morning that beckons before me –
Stirring my mind with mellifluous strains –
Onwards they fly to where moons shower their teardrops
Downwards from Heaven as pearl-polished rain,

Sweeping the cosmos in gleaming crescendos,
Spiralling softly round turrets of dreams,
Sparkling through colonnades hewn out of starlight,
Shooting past filigree, fountain-borne streams,

Fading from sight as the morning now greets me,
Sweeping my dreams from awakening eyes
Far to the evening like pale ghosts of autumn,
Leaving me gazing at bright newborn skies –

Laughing through mirrors of radiant sunlight –
Lighting my life like a scintillant shore
Softly caressed by the ocean's reflections;
New worlds are calling – and dreams are no more.

My street of Yesterday, the subject of this poem, is a side street in Wednesbury, West Midlands, where my grandparents and great-aunts once lived in a small but lovely old house, and where I spent many happy days every year throughout my childhood and teenage years. Although they are all long departed now, whenever I walk down this street today – whether in reality or only in my mind – I never see it as it is, but only as it was – back in those far-off youthful days when it was home to those dear folk who loved me so much.

Yesterday's Street

Along that strangely silent street
Of Yesterday I strolled,
Where humble ragworts gaily tossed
Their joyful heads of gold
Above the gleaming wisps of grass
That peered through pavements worn,
Beneath the silken spider webs
Suspended old and torn
Between the ruddy bricks and slabs
Of broken tumbling walls -
Where oft I watched lithe centipedes
Laboriously crawl
On countless pairs of trembling legs,
As sparrows chattered long,
Or breathlessly in torrents poured
Out eager, scolding songs.

For here, a thriving neighbourhood
Survived through two World Wars,
And from its ceaseless gossiping
There never seemed a pause.
But all things end and soon are lost,
As progress marches on,
For Future has no time for Past,
Its ancient dreams far gone.
And as I watch, a pang vibrates
Within my beating heart,
That all my childhood dreams of Life
Should all too quickly part
Like curtains drifting back through Time,
Till, fading from my sight,
They pass fore'er from Memory
In dismal, clouded flight.

And as the leaves around my feet
In rustling dances whirl,
A tear runs slowly down my cheek
Like some reluctant pearl,
But as I gaze, my memories
Flood quickly back once more.
I see again a tiny house,
And watch its open door
Swing to, as phantoms from my past
Continue on their way,
All unaware of future worlds,
Of other, unborn days,
As like a rushing stream of ghosts
Each vision flashes by,
Recapturing their long-lost forms
Within my watching eye –

Like characters from fairy tales,
Now distant, far, and gone.
For like a living carousel
Our world moves ever on,
Till one fine day we'll see again
Those kingdoms of our past,
And then, like they, as phantoms we
Forever more shall last,
Amidst the world that we knew best,
For all must fade and die,
And pass at last beyond the clear
Blue shadow of the sky.
And as I turn, a last farewell
Upon my ear is cast,
For still my dreams are haunted by
The murmurs of my past.

PART 5:
THE GLORY OF GOD

Nowadays framed and hanging on the wall facing my desk in my study here at home is a poster that was once blue-tacked to the wall in my laboratory at university back in my post-graduate days. It portrays a tiny puma cub, its eyes still unopened, bravely clambering forward. And below the cub is the following quote from Psalm 55:22: "Cast your burden upon the Lord and He will sustain you". During the darkest periods of my life, I have drawn much comfort and strength from that poster, filling me with the certain hope that God will indeed always support and guide me, and reminding me that I need only to look about and listen to affirm that His presence and glory are all around me at all times.

> I have no regret for the Past,
> For the vanished gods.
> The certainty of an Almighty Power,
> Who harmonizes Nature in the equilibrium of His laws,
> Is of greater benefit to my soul than all these dreams.

Madame Michelet – *Nature; Or, The Poetry of Earth and Sea*

> What is the whisper of the dying year?
> "Passing away," it sighs, "Passing away;"
> Nothing below continues in one stay;
> All earthly glories fade and disappear.
> The haunts to childhood and to memory dear,
> The cherished walls where once we knelt to pray,
> Our very churches crumble and decay:
> The tooth of Time corrodeth all things here.
> But 'mid the general wreck two things endure:
> No change shall touch them nor decay shall wrong;
> The steadfast stars may fall; God's Word stands sure;
> And whoso does God's Will, he shall prolong
> His life for ever, in those mansions pure
> Where men shall be as angels bright and strong.

The Rev. Richard Wilton, Rector of Londesborough, East Yorkshire –
'Passing Away; Or, Thoughts For the Last Day of the Year'

Ever since childhood I have adored the fairy tales of Hans Christian Andersen, but I have always questioned whether they were truly intended for children, as many of them seem much too complex, lyrical, and often too dark for young minds to appreciate fully. Over the years, I have adapted a number of them to yield narrative poems, including this one, which is based upon my all-time favourite Andersen story.

The Angel

Day was fading like a phantom
As the evening softly drew
Spangled veils above each village,
And the moon's pale radiance grew.
Stars lit up the sable heavens
With their softly twinkling light,
Like a host of spectral lanterns
From the valleys of the night.

But below their twilit kingdom
Flew a shining image mild –
There, an angel, bearing gently
In its lovely arms a child.
For the child had died that evening,
And the angel bore it long,
As it spoke in blissful murmurs
Like a peaceful, dulcet song:

"When a good child dies, an angel
Flits from Heaven's golden Bliss,
And embraces long this infant
With a warm and tender kiss.
Then it spreads its wings like crescents
Soaring brightly through the sky,
And with joy it takes the infant,
As through all the world they fly,
To the lands where once this youngster
Had found Happiness and Peace,
Where they gather sprigs of flowers
Whose souls then will meet release,
And will bloom with lasting beauty
In the bliss of Heaven's calm.
But the flower the child loved dearest
Will receive a voice of balm,

And will sing with all the angels
Each rejoicing psalm and chord
In a universal chorus
Praising ever more our Lord."

And the youngster listened softly
In a tranquil, peaceful dream,
As they passed through lovely gardens,
Over woodland vales and streams,
To the lands in which the infant
Spent its most delightful hours,
Where they'd stay to gather bouquets
Of the most resplendent flowers.

Here they saw a fragrant rose tree,
Now forgotten, all alone.
For its stem had once been broken
When the buds were but half-grown.
Now they drooped in wilting sadness,
Though the rose was still in bloom,
So enchanting, as it waited
For its end, its final tomb.

And the child sighed long, and murmured:
"Pray, dear Angel, take it too,
So that once again, in Heaven,
It may live and bloom anew."
And the angel kissed the infant,
As it plucked the wilted rose;
And the infant's eyes half-opened,
For they wanted not to close.
Thus they gathered many flowers:
Some were beautiful and fair,
But amidst their sprigs, the lowly
Buttercup was also there.
And the happy child spoke softly:
"We have flowers now," he said.
And the lovely wingèd angel
Smiled, and nodded then his head.

Yet they flew not up to Heaven,
Still remaining in the town,
Which lay sleeping in the shadows
Of the evening's dusky gown.
For they hovered long in silence
O'er a dark and narrow street
Where a rubbish pile lay, trampled
By the shoes of many feet.
And the angel pointed downwards
To a dim, deserted spot
Where a large white flower lay shrivelled
By a broken plaster pot.
For the flower had been discarded,
Thrown away and left to die.
But the angel said: "This also
We shall take, and as we fly
Up to Heaven I shall tell you
Then the story of this flower".
So they onwards flew, as Morning
Lit the dawn's first rosy hour

"There, below," the angel murmured,
"Lived a sick, bedridden boy,
In a cellar where the sunlight
Was his comfort and his joy
When on crutches he could hobble
Round his tiny, darkened room,
As the sun's caressing shaftlets
Filtered softly through its gloom.
And, when on such days he sat there,
Bony fingers thin and red
With the flow of blood within them,
"He's been out," his parents said.

"One fair spring, the neighbour's youngster
Brought a leafy beech tree bough,
Which the poor sick boy would dangle
O'er his head, and wonder how
Bright and happy he would be if
He could sit beneath the trees
In the forest every summer
'Midst the coolness of the breeze.

"Then the neighbour's son collected
Many sprigs of springtime flowers
From the woodlands' verdant arbours
And the valleys' leafy bowers.
And amongst them was a white flower
With its fragile roots preserved,
Which, when watered in a plant pot,
As a small flower garden served.
Thus it flourished, sending blossom
Forth each sunny summer's day,
And it gave him hope and comfort
In its simple humble way.
Soon it entered e'en his dreamworld,
As it bloomed for him alone.
And as e'er he watched, it seemed that
Even fairer had it grown.
For its beauty was his pleasure,
And its spirit was his breath.
And towards his flower, forever,
Still the boy turned, e'en in death.

"For a year the flower had stood there,
Lone, forgotten by the world
When the boy flew up to Heaven
Where a new World lay unfurled.
And when finally his parents
Moved away to other lands,
They forgot the drooping flower, and
So it met with stony hands,
For into the street they threw it,
Like an old and broken toy.
But the happiness and comfort
That it brought to that sick boy
Is the reason we have placed it
In our nosegay with the rest."
And the child was filled with pleasure,
As with wonder was he blessed.

"Yet how knowest you of all this?"
Asked the small, enquiring child.
And the angel answered gently
With a murmur calm and mild:
"Every word I spoke is true, and
Now the answer I shall tell –
For I was myself that sick boy,
Yes, I know my dear flower well."

And the infant's eyes were opened,
Filled with Happiness and Love,
For they then, at that same moment,
Were in Heaven far Above.
And the infant, like the angel,
Now had sweeping snowy wings.
And together flew they softly
Hand in hand, in endless rings,
While, their lives renewed forever,
All their flowers bloomed full of joy.
But the happiest by far was
Still the small flower of the boy,
For it gained a voice in Heaven,
And with blessed delight it sang
With the seraphim forever
As the chimes of Heaven rang.
For the wondrous bliss of Heaven
Stretches on without an end.
And fore'er its peaceful radiance
Shall, to all, God's message send.

But of all God's great creations
Shaped by loving Hands of Power,
None could be more truly happy
Than that white once-withered flower,
Which sang ever to its Father,
For its joy was now complete,
Saved from Death and borne to Glory
From a dark and narrow street.

In this poem, I have sought to manifest in mere words the vibrant, shimmering embodiment of power and joy that is the waterfall, as it must have appeared when newly brought into being by God during the Creation.

As Bright as the Waterfall

A shimmering sparkle of diamonds, so clear,
Cascading and showering crystalline spheres,
Which glisten and glitter like teardrops of dew,
As shadows of gold from the sun filter through.

For high in the mountains is where it was born –
A bright dazzling dancer in God's primal dawn,
Which rocketed downwards in shining array
To herald the coming of God's newborn day.

A fountain erupting in eager delight,
A radiant torrent of luminous light,
Which trickles and tinkles and ricochets higher,
Like glittering arrows of star-spangled fire.

An infinite spirit forever in flight,
Recapturing spectra of transient light
To send forth their beauty reborn and unfurled
In crescents of joy from the Roof of the World.

This poem borrows, adapts, and interweaves a number of separate strands – the legend that the cruciform marking present on every donkey's back was placed there by Jesus in gratitude for being carried by one of their kind during His triumphant procession into Jerusalem on the first Palm Sunday; the idea of that particular donkey being granted immortality, so that it has secretly survived in unchanging form down through all the centuries into the present day; and its chance discovery one Christmas morning by a group of children who have no idea of its origin or significance.

The Christmas Donkey

Christmas drifts silently downwards 'ere Morning
Rises from dreams through the depths of the sky,
Softly caressing each child wrapped in slumber –
Sleeping in peace as the stars twinkle by.

And in a field stands a little brown donkey,
Gazing through Space from an icicled world,
Nuzzling the snow with his soft velvet muzzle,
Shaking its crystals from eyelashes curled.

Now, as he pauses, the dawn flushes brightly,
Blushing like rose petals strewn from Above,
Waking the children with murmurs from Morning,
Carolling joyfully anthems of Love.

Soon they chase merrily into the garden,
And as they sing of what Christmas will yield,
One of them points to the little brown donkey,
Standing alone in the snow-covered field.

Swiftly they race through the shimmering snowflakes,
Up to his paddock with eager delight,
Each to embrace him with warm, tender kisses,
Melting the snow in its spiralling flight.

And as he brays in the midst of the children,
Gaily they deck him with tinsel and flowers –
Joyfully plucked from their Christmas tree's branches –
Glistening brightly in colourful showers.

But as the heavens' first frost-killing sunlight
Glints from each bauble and gleams from each boss,
Softly a shadow falls over his shoulders,
Sombre and still in the shape of a Cross.

And as he stands there, a tear trickles slowly
Down through his lashes in sorrowful flight,
As he remembers through centuries countless,
Whom he'd once carried with love and delight.

Palms and hosannas regaled him in triumph,
There on his back sat our Saviour and Lord,
Smiling and nodding to people and children,
Standing all round in a vast, cheering horde.

"Why did they spurn Him, betray Him, and kill Him –
Nailed to that Cross and then left there to die?"
Still the poor donkey weeps long at the memory,
Held for Eternity deep in his eyes.

And as the children, not seeing his sorrow,
Run away laughing, the donkey's warm heart
Burns with a passionate love so intense that
Not e'en the chill of the icicles' darts

E'er could refrigerate, e'er could extinguish,
Burning in silence this cold Christmas Day,
Lingering still, like the Cross's dark shadow –
Borne from a green hill so far, far away.

The symbolic association of the poppy with the remembrance of those who fought and fell during wartime is very potent, and is one that I sought to capture and honour in the following poem – my own tribute to those brave heroes who gave their lives so that we could live ours. May we never forget them, and the sacrifice that they made for all of us.

Fields of Remembrance

Far through the countryside's languorous dreaming
Strolled I one morning in summertime past,
Wondering why this enrapturing vista
Couldn't unchanging forever more last.

And as I gazed o'er its velvet-gowned valleys,
There lay a poppy field, burnished and bright;
Scarlet heads tossing on stems green and slender,
Swaying round ever to meet the sun's light.

Crimson and fiery as dancing infernos,
Eyes filled with darkness like eveningtide's shades,
Peering through petals emblazoned with ruby,
Outwards forever to sunlight displayed.

And as I stood there, their message came softly,
Brought by the zephyr on swift wings of Love;
For, as I listened, their spirits drew nearer,
Borne 'neath the cloudbanks of Heaven above.

E'en though they spoke without words, without voices,
Eyes sparkling brightly from tall fiery heads,
Theirs was a message more real, yet more distant,
Stranger than any before – for they said:

"We are the spirits of those who for Freedom
Gave up their lives in the struggle of War.
We are reborn in the world they created,
Shedding the tears and the ills that they bore."

And as I watched them, their petals drooped downwards,
Burdened with dewdrops, each tender and clear,
Capturing memories borne through all ages,
Living again in each poppy-shed tear.

Theirs was a love more intense, more consuming,
Than could be ever disrupted by War;
Peace was their dream and their only ambition,
This was their goal – this is what they died for.

And as I left, still their beauty burnt brighter,
Bright as the sun scorching upwards and higher;
Ne'er would their courage and hope be forgotten,
Cherished fore'er in the poppies' bright fire,

Burning fore'er in the hearts of all mankind
Living in peace after violence and War.
Freedom has come to this fair English country:
This was their dream – this is what they fought for.

As with 'The Angel', the following poem was inspired by a beautifully-written short story (entitled 'The Bell') by Hans Christian Andersen – one of my poetry's most influential muses.

Heaven's Bell

Morning rose slowly through pale, dreaming cloudlets,
Peering down softly from clear, violet skies,
Watching the countryside waking from slumber,
Sending forth sunlight from warm golden eyes.

And as the song of the warbling dawn chorus
Drifted in ripples of carolling darts,
Church bells pealed gaily their glorious chansons,
Born from the joy of their bright, silver hearts.

Yet, 'midst the chimes of their vibrant crescendo,
Echoed the sound of a more distant bell,
Deep and majestic in strange, holy splendour,
Singing unseen through each woodland and dell.

Rich was its tone, like a solemn concerto
Borne from a World of Perfection and Truth,
Calling me onwards through dingle and forest,
Haunting the wandering soul of my youth.

Snow-white anemones listened in silence,
Bowing down low as its heavenly chimes
Rang out before me in infinite glory,
Growing more fair with the passage of Time.

And as I walked through viridian woodlands,
Lilac convolvuli trumpeted long,
While from the arbours the bell's regal chorus
Softly resounded through hyacinth throngs.

Still I continued, past silver-lit lakesides,
And as the swans drifted softly from sight,
Leaving their shadows on deep turquoise waters,
Far up ahead shone a shimmering light.

And as I passed through the lavender mountains,
Seeking the bell that had called from afar,
Fountains danced brightly from woodland to valley,
Spraying the vales with a bright shower of stars.

Meadows lay glistening on in the distance,
Dappled with poppies in slumbering bliss,
Peacefully dreaming in rapturous beauty,
Wrapped in enchantment by Summer's soft kiss.

And as I climbed to the grey, cloudy summit,
Sunset spread softly through brilliant skies,
Filling the world with its rosy suffusion,
Scorching with colour my wondering eyes.

And as the sun sank down softly through Heaven,
There, 'neath the sky, lay the glittering sea,
Snaring the sun's silhouetted reflection –
Here, if at all, would the bell surely be.

Lo! What magnificence! Lo! What resplendence!
There stood the sun like an altar of gold,
Raised o'er the sea as a shimmering halo,
Kissed by the ocean's voluptuous folds.

Here was the wondrous Cathedral of Nature –
Pillars of willow, and Heaven its dome,
Singing of Beauty, of Love in the Highest,
Borne from the chorus of wavelet and foam.

Stars twinkled brightly like crystalline lanterns,
Lighting up softly the pathways of Night,
Casting their shadows like glittering diamonds
Down to the woodlands in crescents of light.

And, as I stood 'neath the Archway of Heaven,
Nature and Poetry singing as one,
Still the invisible Bell rang above me,
Calling me ever more, upwards and on,

Singing of God, of His Power and His Promise,
Sending His Love in melodious chords,
Borne by the souls of the Blessèd forever –
Praise in excelsis, for theirs is the Lord!

I remember my mother recounting to me as a small child the biblical story of how, after the Great Deluge had ceased, God set in the sky the first rainbow, to signify His promise that never again would He flood the world. In this poem about a typical rainy day, I have sought to convey and contrast the rain's frenetic haste with the serene and holy glory of the rainbow that follows sedately in its wake.

Here Comes Another Rainy Day

Hear the noisy splashing of the rain upon the ground,
Gushing and emitting great cacophonies of sound.
Racing down the windows at a giddy, speeding pace,
Fluid sprinters chasing in an everlasting race.

Grey clouds hang in clusters o'er a dark, deserted town,
Streets lie bare and empty as the rain keeps pouring down,
People sitting snugly in their homes, close by the fire,
Watching scarlet flames that dart up through the air and higher.

Still the rain beats downwards, flooding roads and drowning streets,
Swooping down the avenues on liquid wingtips fleet.
Torrents team in gay delight from windowsill and spout,
All so full of movement that their very souls fly out.

Trees are hung in raindrops, dripping down their diamonds bright,
Gleaming, clear, and shining, and reflecting coloured light,
Toppling from the branches, rushing down, and then they're gone,
Soon replaced by others to repeat what they have done.

Small flowers spring up more enchanting, fresher than before,
Filled with new life, filled with beauty, up and up they soar,
Bursting with new energy, renewed by wind and rain,
Now to grow more lovely, bringing happiness again.

Soon the storm is over, and the clouds roll back in awe –
Here's the rainbow, promising that rain will come no more.
Veiling all the darkness with its dazzling, sparkling arc,
Light has come, reborn again from out of storm and dark,

Shining like an archway leading to a Second World –
One that, to our mortal eyes, has never been unfurled.
Darts of light shoot forth in streaming, multicoloured flight –
To a world of Darkness, God has brought the gift of Light.

How strange it is that whereas the seconds of our lives pass quite slowly, the minutes seem to go by faster, and the hours faster still, as our lives race ever onward to their conclusion. And yet as they depart, others commence – the one certainty in a world of uncertainly is that Life, in an innumerable multitude of forms, is ever-present.

Life – The Infinity of the World

The throbbing fingers of a clock
Tick slowly by, ne'er ceasing,
Just as Time moves on forever,
Never stopping, never easing,
In its swift, eternal race
Through the vales of Outer Space.

Seconds trickle by like raindrops
In my life, so little being,
Followed closely by the minutes
As they chase, forever fleeing,
Through the heavens still and grey
In the silhouette of Day –

Like a windmill turning softly
Through a timeless, depthless pool,
As its orbit circles ever
Round its lone, immortal spool,
Till it sinks away to die
In the caverns of the sky.

Thus my life flits swiftly onwards
As the hours soon drop away
Like a host of cloudy phantoms,
Growing fainter every day,
Till at last their forms are gone,
And the Future marches on –

Like a journey hoping ever
For a journey of its own,
As its unknown dreams await me,
Each I meet but once, alone.
Then it's gone, it cannot wait,
Nor can any ghost of Fate,

Till, to God, my soul turns humbly
On my final mortal day.
Metamorphosis is over,
And my spirit flies away,
To a Land of lasting Peace,
Where e'en Time shall find release.

Here the mole symbolises dark introspection, shunning the light and God, whereas the fieldmouse symbolises bright outward wonder, seeking the light and God.

The Mole and the Fieldmouse

Morning tossed her starlit bonnet
Far across the glinting waters,
Calling softly through the heavens
To the hours, her shining daughters,
Bidding all a fond awakening
From the shades of Evening's gloaming,
Flitting past on rainbow wingtips
Far away to oceans foaming,

Passing by a tiny fieldmouse
Gazing through the dreaming havens,
Watching Sleep drift back through shadows
Open-winged like silent ravens.
Still he watched, and softly wondered
What beyond his own existence
Held the world in sparkling fingers,
Staring far into the distance.

Yet beneath his earthen chateaux
Groped a mole in velvet blindness –
His was Darkness, Night eternal,
Void of Light, of warmth, of kindness,
Caring not for worlds beyond him,
Seeking only deep beginnings,
Roots of tree and grass and mountain,
Curling downwards, twisting, spinning.

But the mouse sought Light and Wisdom,
Moving through the golden morning,
Past his fields and sun-drenched meadows
Kissed by Day, while gently yawning,
Listening long to fairy laughter
'Neath a sapphire-mirrored ceiling,
Shot with love-lit shafts from Heaven
Till his heart with joy lay reeling
Far beyond his lowly meadows,
Blessed by God in glory reigning,
As he scampered ever onward
Through a land of peace unwaning.

On he roamed, past lake and fountain,
'Neath their showers of starlit winglets –
Crystal spirits silver-shining,
Casting far their sparkling ringlets.
Birds flew past like fleeting ripples
Through their world of bright reflection;
There the mouse paused long in wonder,
Lost 'midst such divine perfection.
And as Morning bowed to Noontide,
Oceans sang from distant shingle,
Borne from half-forgotten dreaming
Where their waves e'er intermingle.

Theirs were murmurs drawn from sadness,
Empty songs from future dawnings;
Theirs were dreams from sleepy shorelines
Crossed by pale, departed mornings.
And above these lonely islets
Diamond stars hung softly winking,
Peering far through timeless windows,
Lantern-shining, dewdrop-twinkling.
Night had come, unseen, unnoticed,
Lulling all with dulcet singing,
As her train of shrouded shadows
Through the ebbing skies were winging.

Still he sat among the starlight,
'Neath the moon's pellucid crescent –
Like an archway spanning Heaven,
Hewn from Space, and iridescent
With the silence of the cosmos,
Like a lifetime silver-streaming
Through the cobwebs of the future,
Past the gloomy planets dreaming
As they spin in spiralled orbits
Far away into the distance,
Till at last they meet their other
From a parallel existence.

Then, as one, they die together
Like a shadow kissed by Dawning;
Thus they pass from Time forever,
Leaving Space to grieve in mourning.
Whispers echo out to nowhere
In a vastness never-ending,
All-consuming, all-demanding,
As its light sweeps, ever wending
Through the corridors of Wisdom
To the hearts of all who hearken.
And for those their dreams shall flourish,
And their souls shall never darken.

Thus the mouse found Inspiration
'Midst those hours of twilit rapture;
And he knew his heart could never
Hope to understand or capture
All the wealth of God's great Wisdom,
Though his soul with joy was burnished,
As it ever brimmed with passion
And with happiness was furnished.
But his heart had met with beauty
And the love that conquers sorrow.
These had filled his mind with Wisdom,
And the hope in each Tomorrow.

Then he turned away, for Nature
Softly called her tiny foundling,
And he scurried far through Evening
To his home and his surroundings.
Yet his eyes shone much more brightly,
Each a pool of moonlight beaming,
For within their liquid darkness
Still the stars of Space lay gleaming.

But the mole sought not the starlight,
Nor for him the gold of Morning;
Sun and moon held no enchantment,
Nor the rosy hues of Dawning.
In his heart was nothing joyful,
Wonderment and love were lacking;
He cared only for the earth, through
Whose dark realm his soul was tracking.

So the mole dug ever downwards,
Till with Ignorance he stumbled;
And he died amid the darkness,
And his spirit fled and crumbled.
Those who live in vales of Shadow
Never hear Light's joyful laughter,
Just as those with hearts of Darkness
Ne'er will see a new Hereafter.

It was my mother who introduced me to the evocative light-classical compositions of English composer Albert Ketèlbey (1875-1959). Many of his best-loved compositions were thematic, such as 'In a Chinese Temple Garden', 'In a Persian Market', 'In the Mystic Land of Egypt', and perhaps his most famous work of all, 'In a Monastery Garden'. It was while listening to this lovely composition one afternoon that the idea came for the following poem, which I duly wrote while the strains of Ketèlbey's music played on, inspiring and shaping it into its final form.

The Monastery Garden

Out of the nightmare of War's raging battle
Struggled two soldiers away from the field,
Walking in silence so far from their homeland,
Hoping that somewhere a vision would yield,

One that would show them why War must continue,
Why they must struggle when all else seems lost,
Why so much bloodshed should lie over Europe,
Death being Victory's ultimate cost.

And as they wandered, they heard from a clearing
Singing and psalms drifting softly all round,
As in the branches a nightingale's lilting
Filled all the vales with melodious sound.

There, up ahead, lay a monastery's garden,
Golden and peaceful in sun-dappled bliss;
Fountains danced brightly in dazzling crescendos,
Flowers stretched up longing for sunlight's warm kiss.

Here the two paused, looking into the garden;
Then to the gate they approached side by side,
Gazed for a time, and, refreshed by its beauty,
Opened it slowly and entered inside.

And in the wonder and peace of the garden,
Each sat there thinking of all that was past,
Knowing that they could reshape the world's future,
Knowing that freedom forever could last.

Blossom fell gently upon the two soldiers,
Fragrant and fragile as transient dreams,
Bringing them sleep to escape from the fighting,
Hiding War's shadow with Light's golden beams.

And in their dream stood an Angel of Mercy,
Towering over the spectres of War,
Till, when his countenance gazed on these phantoms,
Each one was shrivelled, and War was no more.

Now, when they woke, they possessed a new wisdom,
Knowing at last what their fighting must bring;
Blessed with new Hope 'midst Despair's cloak of Panic,
Hearing the churchbells for Victory ring.

And as they sat there, they talked of the battle,
Each one now conquering War's bitter Dread.
Then, as the first paused in thought for a moment,
Up stood the other in silence, and said:

"Never has so much been lost by so many,
Lost in the dream of a kingdom of Peace,
Hoping their sons will be born into Freedom,
Praying that by their own deaths War will cease.

"Never again must our world be divided,
Fighting in vain for the pleasure of War;
Next time the war will not end with our dying,
Next time our world will be lost ever more."

Then they walked slowly away from the garden,
Back to the fighting, the guns, and the war.
Yet they knew not of the Presence who watched them,
For they looked back not, and so never saw

There in the garden an Angel stood softly –
He who had sent them their vision of Peace –
Watching them go to a world draped in Sorrow,
Doomed till their fighting could bring them release.

And as they vanished, the Seraph spoke softly:
"Eden was lost to you, children of Greed;
Never again must such war come to being,
Next time from Woe you will never be freed.

"Next time your fighting will be your destruction,
Mankind will wither, and Mankind will die.
And of the world left polluted with Evil,
Only a mushroom will rise through the sky."

I have previously mentioned that René Magritte's remarkable painting 'The Voice of the Winds' inspired two very different poems of mine. Its memorable title gave rise to my own poem of that same title, included in Part 2 of this present book; but its image, that of three huge airborne spheres, captivated my mind until at last I penned the following verses.

The Music of the Spheres

Lilting music from the heavens
Sailing endlessly through Space.
Legendary, its song is ne'er heard,
Lifting high, its rhythms race,
Filled with happiness and tears –
The strange music of the spheres.

Sailing past the shining stars and
Through the convexes of Time,
Sweet and silent is its music,
Flowing on in dulcet rhyme,
Hope its bearer, Peace its wings,
Touching every living thing.

Reaching golden realms beyond us,
Never strident, never shrill,
Blending peacefully together,
Music soft, and music still –
Melodies from sacred lands
Past the rainbow's coloured bands.

On it plays, unending paeans
Of great happiness and bliss,
And our world stands still in wonder
As all Time becomes a kiss,
Symbolising Hope and Love
From our Father up Above.

Still this silent lilting music
Flows forever to our lives,
Yet we never hear its message,
For instead we always strive
To rule everything we see,
Crushing all till all must flee.

But for mankind there is hope still
Of a free and better land,
Where all lives can live together,
And will form a single hand –
Pointing up, where all will hear
The strange music of the spheres.

There are many traditional, quite often poignant religious folktales featuring animals, some of which are well known, others less so. In the following poem, I have combined two of these age-old stories - the famous legend of how the robin gained its red breast, and the less familiar legend of how the crossbill acquired its twisted beak.

The Robin and the Crossbill

A tall wooden Cross cast its pitiless shadow
Across a green hill 'neath the grey, leaden sky.
For mankind had crucified Jesus, its Saviour,
And left Him there helpless to suffer and die.

But two tiny birds came to visit Lord Jesus,
Two small humble creatures with hearts full of love.
The little brown robin and bright crimson crossbill,
Each blessed by the Light of their Father Above.

When Jesus looked down and beheld the small robin,
He smiled at him softly, and down from His breast
His blood trickled slowly like deep scarlet teardrops,
And falling below stained the robin's white chest.

The crossbill in vain used his bill to remove the
Cruel nails that impaled Jesus' hands and His feet,
But prised with such force that his bill crossed and twisted
'Ere, strength being spent, he conceded defeat.

And e'er since that day when they visited Jesus,
The bill of each crossbill is twisted and curled,
While Jesus' red blood on each robin's chest lingers,
Reminding us just how much God loves our world.

In the Kalevala epic of Finnish mythology, Tuonela is the island of the dead, encircled by a black river upon which a spectral swan swims, calling out mournfully – a scene captured beautifully by Finnish composer Jean Sibelius's haunting composition, 'The Swan of Tuonela', in which the swan is perfectly represented by the cor anglais. Listening to its plaintive melody one day, I wrote the following poem, but I chose to transform Tuonela's supernatural swan from an apparition of doom into a messenger of hope.

The Swan of Tuonela

Far away lies Tuonela –
Land of Twilight, world of Death –
Draped in mournful, shrouded shadows
Cold as Evening's chilling breath.

And encompassing this island
Flows a river black as Night,
For it carries no reflection,
Shunning every form of light.

But upon its sable waters
Drifts a swan in snowy pride,
Calling softly through the darkness
As the river's ripples ride

'Neath its outstretched wings in silence
While it sings it strange refrain,
And the zephyr bears it lightly,
So that all may hear its strain.

For the Swan of Tuonela,
At the world's far-distant end,
Sings of Light in realms of Shadow,
And fore'er its message sends

Out to all in need of Courage,
Telling all to strive anew.
For the Star of Hope in Heaven
Will forever more shine through,

And will guide us with the promise
Of our Lord's undying Love,
Till our souls return forever
To that shining Star Above.

Certain religious stories, such as St George and the Dragon, have generated very considerable interest down through the centuries and have been profusely celebrated in the arts and literature. In stark contrast, however, there are others that have attracted much less notice, yet are no less memorable. The following story is one of these hitherto-neglected Christian legends, which has stayed in my mind ever since I first read it many years ago, so I finally decided to retell it in verse.

The Transformation of Saint Eustacius

Through the emerald forests
Of golden-hued Dawn,
Rode Eustacius, a soldier
Of Rome, one fine morn,
As his hounds bayed all round him
With dark, fearful eyes,
Like a torrent of shadows
'Neath newly-born skies.

So the soldier rode onward
Through golden-leaved trees,
While the hounds' dismal howling
Still hung on the breeze
Like a dream half-forgotten
'Twixt Future and Past –
Yet still doomed by its maker
Forever to last.

Then ahead of Eustacius
A white stag appeared,
And the soldier's steed trembled,
Then, shivering, reared.
Just as if the stag's presence
Imbued it with awe,
As the hunter peered onwards
And then, the deer, saw.

All at once, the stag stiffened,
Then fled through the trees,
But Eustacius pursued it,
Through clearings and leas.
On he chased this white wonder,
Past mountains and vales,
And the morn became noontide
In forests and dales.

Later, Evening drew gently
The curtains of Night
Far across the blue heavens,
Now dappled with light
From the glistening stars set
In countless array,
Each a tiny eye peering
Through blankets of grey.

And as they witnessed softly
The hunt far below,
E'en the moon wept in sadness,
And shrouded its glow
To give cover of darkness
'Midst shadowy glades
To the hunted stag, weary
As still the hounds bayed.

But the stag was now tiring,
Its head dangled low,
As its heart heaved and pounded,
Its eyes full of woe,
Till it sank down exhausted
On carpets of dew,
As the hounds' ghastly howling
More terrible grew.

Then Eustacius perceived it,
Stretched outwards to die,
As its fragile heart throbbed 'neath
The sorrowful sky.
And the stag watched the soldier
With eyes dark and mild,
For it made no swift movement,
Yet cried like a child.

Then a pale shaft of moonlight
Fell softly from Space,
And its shimmering beauty
Lit up the deer's face.
And as all the world waited,
The stag raised its head.
Its mouth opened, and then, with
A human voice, said:

"Why dost thou still pursueth
Me long through the trees?
I am Christ," as Eustacius
Dropped low to his knees.
For the stag was surrounded
By radiant light,
Like a star incandescent
That passed from all sight

To the heavens resplendent
In Glory Divine.
Then Eustacius looked up, and
Drew slowly the Sign
Of the Cross there before him –
A new saint was born,
In the reincarnation
Of God's golden Dawn.

How many times – countless, assuredly – has the question forming the title of this poem been asked and pondered over by thinkers of every nation across the globe and through all the ages of human existence? Here are my own thoughts.

What is God?

Lone I sat upon a mountain
Captured long by silent thought.
"What is God?" I wondered softly,
As illusions round me fought

To attract my mind's attention
While I sat beneath the skies.
And the hush of peace drew slowly
O'er this cloudy world of sighs.

For the Voice of God was present –
Not the clamour of alarm,
Or the roar of wreaking earthquakes,
Just a quiet Voice of Calm.

"What is God?" I wondered, seeking
One who ne'er to me has lied.
And my Conscience answered softly –
"I am God," its voice replied.

"I am God within each mortal.
I – who speaks amid the fire.
I – the diamond in the darkness.
I – the rose upon the briar,

"Leading all who live untempted
By the guiling tones of Harm,
Or the cunning wiles of Hatred,
Or by Envy's bitter charm.

"I am He Who walks unnoticed
In sweet Virtue's world of balm,
And the isles of Hope and Freedom;
I – a quiet Voice of Calm."

And as Night with veils of Shadow
Cloaked the sunset splashed with red,
I at last knew what my God was:
"I am God," my Conscience said.

For me, 'Fantasia on Greensleeves' by Ralph Vaughan Williams conjures forth the beauty of the English countryside like no other piece of music that I've ever heard. So it was that one day, while listening yet again to its glorious, heart-stirring melody, I penned the following poem, suffused with the verdant spirit of Nature that pours from every note of that sublime musical composition.

The Wild Roses

As roses bloom in leafy briars,
Their fragrant scent drifts ever higher,
Through sunlit clouds and heavens bright
To Lands beyond all mortal sight,

Reflecting in their mellow stare
The countryside of England fair –
The seas of ruffling meadow grass
Through which the breezy day-winds pass,

The shady woodlands, deep and cool,
A shining, rippling forest pool,
The soft blue depth of western skies
Through which a summer swallow flies,

The tranquil peace of moonlit hours
As starlight dapples sleeping flowers,
And Dawn's rebirth in eastern skies
From misty clouds of dreams and sighs.

All born again in petals curled,
To all their lovely forms unfurled,
In this green English wonderland,
Too fair for us to understand.

Yet gaze we o'er our countryside,
Its splendour deep, its borders wide,
And dream of beauty pure and real,
And in our hearts we softly kneel

In awe and wonder, as we hear
God's shining Voice, so true and clear,
Foretelling days when we shall see
The glory of Eternity.

There are wonders to experience everywhere in this world that God created if we only allow Him to show us, but even these will fade into insignificance compared to those that we shall witness when Fate unfurls before us the glory of God's own World.

Wonders Untold

Snowflakes and butterflies,
Star-spangled streams,
Dewdrops and fireflies,
Pale hazy dreams,
Lanterns bright, doves of white,
Blooms mauve, red, and gold;
Beautiful hints are these
Of wonders untold.

Blue isles of mystery,
Mermaid lagoons,
Nightingale lullabies,
Arching festoons,
Fairy glades, dappling shades,
Moonstones soft and white,
Crimson-tailed falling stars
Exploding in flight.

Facets of memories
Distant and past,
None may forever more
In this world last.
But when Fate's curtains great
Silently unfold,
We shall through reborn eyes
See wonders untold.

PART 6:
YOUNGER DAYS

Childhood was a very special, magical, idyllic time for me, and it inspired this section's poems, all of which I have written specifically for a youthful – or at least a young at heart – audience.

A boat, beneath a sunny sky
Lingering onward dreamily
In an evening of July –

Children three that nestle near,
Eager eye and willing ear
Pleased a simple tale to hear –

Long has paled that sunny sky:
Echoes fade and memories die:
Autumn frosts have slain July.

Still she haunts me, phantomwise,
Alice moving under skies
Never seen by waking eyes.

Children yet, the tale to hear,
Eager eye and willing ear,
Lovingly shall nestle near.

In a Wonderland they lie,
Dreaming as the days go by,
Dreaming as the summers die:

Ever drifting down the stream –
Lingering in the golden gleam –
Life, what is it but a dream?

Lewis Carroll – *Through the Looking Glass*

In 1956, French film-maker Albert Lamorisse directed a short but enchanting film entitled 'Le Ballon Rouge' ('The Red Balloon'), which featured a small Parisian boy (played by the director's own son, Pascal) who encountered a large red balloon that seemed to have a life and will of its own. Tragically, a gang of bullies saw the boy with it, pursued them, and finally burst the balloon, only for a host of other balloons all over Paris to break free of their strings and rescue the boy by lifting him up into the sky and carrying him safely away on a breathtaking flight above the rooftops of the city. I saw this poignant but delightful film as a child, when it was shown on British television during the late 1960s, and its magic remained with me long afterwards, giving me the idea for a children's poem about a balloon, but written as if it were almost a living entity.

The Balloon

Like an animated bubble
Bobbing gaily through the sky,
Nodding happily to cloudlets
As it gently dances by.

Spinning swiftly o'er the meadows,
Just a merry, bouncing clown,
Bowing joyfully to Heaven
As it spirals up and down.

Soon it whirls amidst the woodlands,
Here a gaudy, twirling sphere
Rolling slowly down the branches
Like a bright, gigantic tear.

Then some splinters stroke it softly
As around the trees it wends,
But their fond embrace is fatal,
And its life is at an end –

Bursting loudly into pieces;
But, as hours so swiftly pass,
Who will miss a merry bubble
Lying dead amongst the grass?

Seeking to portray in words alone the light, fragile, multicoloured nature of a butterfly, and its fond association with the summer, is no easy task (and which is why I have made two separate attempts! – see also 'Papillon' later in this same section). So please forgive me for cheating so blatantly with the rhyme at the end of the following poem's final line!

The Butterfly

Butterfly, butterfly, hearken to me,
Flitting so gaily, so pretty and free,
Tell me of places to which you have been,
Tell me of wonderful sights that you've seen.

Fair little bringer of bright sunny hours,
Gliding among all the nectar-filled flowers,
Fluttering lightly on gossamer wings,
Soft as the songs that the summer wind sings.

Wings of resplendence, so thin and so frail,
Yet o'er the treetops you dance and you sail,
Wings painted red, flashing purple and blue,
Each its own masterpiece, perfect and true.

Summer suns shimmer and summer suns die;
To warmer countries migrating birds fly.
But when the sun returns, dear butterfly,
Visit my world, do not flutter me by.

These are two of my earliest poems for children, and both are written from a child's point of view. The first is a simple poem of praise to God. The second is a tribute to my brother, André, who in 1955 died when only five weeks old. He was buried on 9 December – four years later, on that very same day, I was born.

The Church

I walked into the church one day,
I felt the need to kneel and pray.
So many things were wrong for me,
The reason why I couldn't see.

I sat inside and looked around,
The church lay still, without a sound.
The altar, aisle, and pews of wood,
The building housing all that's good.

So many ways of serving Him,
Through study, work, and hating sin,
A prayer to give both help and love
To all who live, for God Above.

The Churchyard

The churchyard lies so calm and still,
The church is mounted on a hill.
And in the churchyard, bluebells wild
With daisies sway in cool winds mild.

The long grass growing all around
Soon covers all the soft grey ground,
While bird song breaks the silent air,
As people do in murmured prayer.

And many, through the years, pass through,
But some remain, my brother too.
His name – André – was all I knew,
God wanted him, and Jesus too.

Fireworks can be very beautiful, but also very dangerous – and it was in order to alert children to this potentially deadly combination that I wrote this poem.

Fireworks – Bright Flowers of the Night

Look – bright flowers of the night!
What a wonderful sight!
The rockets, the sparklers, and flares.
A shower of stars,
As if sent from Mars,
People laughing, forgetting their cares.

The bonfire burns brightly,
The chestnuts roast slightly,
The smoke rises blue in the air.
Guy Fawkes on the fire,
The flames rising higher,
And all of the family are there.

But while all this goes on:
"Please remember, my son,
That danger is lurking out there."
My mother gives warning:
"Night's followed by morning,
There are some things I cannot repair."

The purpose of this poem is to demonstrate to children that just because something is small, this does not automatically mean that it is of little importance, worthy only of being ignored or forgotten. In other words, good things very often do come in small packages – and remember, even the smallest of things has a reason for being here.

The Forget-Me-Not

Forget-me-not, for I am small,
Yet I still grow where others fall.
So blue, so true, with petals five;
Sweet hope that keeps our world alive.

Forget-me-not, for I am but
A poor wild flower, yet I was put
Upon His Earth, with man and beast
To live in peace when Spring's released.

Forget-me-not, though small I stand,
A tiny life in giant lands.
For though through taller plants I grope.
Where'er I grow, there too grows hope.

Despite its destructive nature, I've always had a soft spot for this small burrowing mammal. Consequently, I have attempted to show to children via this poem that even an animal as seemingly insignificant and rarely-seen in our world as the mole can be a creature of importance, a veritable king, in its own specialised realm.

The Mole

Velvet King of Underground,
Sending skywards earthy mounds
In the search for hidden worms,
Deep below the ground so firm.

Small is he, with tiny ears,
For below he seldom hears
Horses neigh, or church bells ring,
Thunderstorms, or songbirds sing.

Velvet King, yet blind he goes,
Tunnelling where nothing grows.
Inky black, no sound or light
Breaks this dark, eternal night.

Still he digs through soil, for Earth –
Who, to all life, once gave birth –
Pledged a world of endless holes
To its King, the velvet mole.

Time-slips are fascinating if baffling concepts, which I have utilised in this story poem. Although I haven't stated it explicitly, I'm sure you'll realise that instead of the monk being in the distant past (as the child narrating this poem assumes), in reality he is in the distant future, because the finding of the Cross after meeting the monk inspires the child to become a monk – the monk. *In other words, the monk that the child meets is himself, as he will become in the future.*

The Monastery

One pleasant country afternoon
Through lonely woods I strolled,
When hazy mists began to fall
In swirling cloudy folds
And blinded every beam of light,
None penetrating through,
Until at last the mists dispersed,
And rose through skies of blue.

I looked around, and then I saw
A monastery, concealed
By glades of trees and tiny flowers
That edged each greening field.
A pretty garden lay all round
The monastery, so fair
With trees in blossom, budding flowers,
Whose sweet scent filled the air.

And high above, unseen by all,
A singing nightingale,
Whose liquid trills and lilting notes
Sailed through each wooded vale.
Sing sweetly, little philomel,
Bring happiness to all –
Shy minstrel of the dusky night,
Of silent eveningfall.

And through this garden walked a monk,
A prayer book in his hand.
He heard the nightingale, and smiled
To hear the merry band
Of feathered singers in the trees,
As thrushes joined the choir,
Till warbling music filled the air
As breezes sent it higher.

And velvet bumblebees buzzed near
Each nectar-brimming flower,
While gaily-spotted ladybirds
Flew by from bloom to bower.
And as he saw each tiny life,
The monk's heart filled with joy,
As he remembered happy days
When he was once a boy –

A quiet boy who loved God's works
Of beauty, true and mild.
And so his life he gave to God,
To seek our Lord's paths mild.
But now he turned, and passed from sight
Beyond the shadowed trees,
And then another mist appeared,
Upon the evening breeze.

And when it lifted from my eyes,
The monastery had gone.
And as for garden, glades, and flowers,
Of these there now was none.
For all were ghosts from other times,
Those realms of glades and moss.
But then, beneath a grassy bower,
I spied a golden Cross –

The Cross that hung around the neck
Of that mild monk I saw.
A Sign that spanned the straits of Time
To lie on grass before
A silent child in country lanes
Whose youthful fears now thawed.
Yes, blessed are the pure in heart,
For they shall see the Lord.

The personification of Nature, as Mother Nature, seemed an excellent theme for a children's poem, so here is my impression of how she might be.

Mother Nature

Mother Nature's in her garden,
Weaving wings of butterflies,
Spinning threads of shining gossamer
From memories and sighs.

In her lap is sparkling stardust,
In her lap are sunbeams bright,
In her lap are moonlit crescents,
Radiating milky light.

In her hair are woven rainbows,
Mauve and lemon, blue and lime,
In her face is love and kindness,
In her eyes is endless Time.

She will change as she is noticed,
No-one ever sees the same.
They see only what their hearts do,
What they see no-one can name.

She lives in her favourite garden,
Maybe yours, or maybe mine.
It need not be royal or regal,
Where rare blossoms intertwine.

It could be a lowly backyard,
Only daisies growing there.
But if honest people love it,
Mother Nature will be there.

For her garden is where goodness
Lives in sympathetic minds
Filled with tenderness and kindness.
Yes, it's here where you will find

Mother Nature – in her garden,
Weaving wings of butterflies,
Spinning threads of shining gossamer,
From memories and sighs.

Representing Sleep and Nod as entities was the inspiration for writing this poem. Years later, I discovered that Walter de la Mare had also written a poem featuring Nod as a person, but, happily, he and I had pursued quite different paths in penning our respective versions.

Nod

Far through Sleep's misty world he goes,
Goes Nod, her old dream-herd.
His paths lie past all waking hours,
Or any spoken word.

With clouded eyes of other worlds
And hair like rippling snow,
He grasps his crook in silken hands,
As onward e'er he'll go.

He lives beyond the realms of men,
Beyond the light of Day.
Yet all have seen him in their sleep
'Midst Slumber's golden ray.

They climb Sleep's purple hills and meet
Her dreams like lambs of white,
And see the swan of Memory,
'Ere Dawn transforms to Light.

But when they wake, Nod disappears,
And ne'er is seen by day.
For where he goes through sunlit hours
No-one can ever say.

Yet through Sleep's misty world he'll go,
Will Nod, her old dream-herd,
Till Night is Light forever, then
Shall Peace fore'er be heard.

Here is my second attempt at capturing the delicate essence of the butterfly in verse.

Papillon

Summertime, and English lime
And lilac butterflies fly free.
But in France, where'er I glance,
As papillons you flit past me.

Papillon, bright papillon,
So small and fragile summer long.
Gold and green, with orange sheen,
You fly through summer's gilded song.

Papillon, fair papillon,
From blooms and buds you dip and rise.
Zephyrs swift you ride, and lift
Your slender thorax to the skies.

Papillon, sweet papillon,
On painted wings you flutter by.
Though so small, you bring to all
The beauty of a butterfly.

The Polperro of this poem is not the picturesque Cornish fishing village of longstanding fame, but is instead the name of the house in which I was born and lived as a child. And its small but beautiful garden, created by my mother, is the garden described here, my own special wonderland in which I spent countless happy hours playing. This poem was written a fair few years ago, and now the garden is gone, but it will live on forever in my memory – and whenever I read these verses, which I wrote specifically for children, I am instantly transported back to that magical world of my childhood. So I hope that if any of today's children do read them, they too will share some of the wonder and joy that this humble little garden and its figures brought to me, even after the tragic event described here.

Polperro

In a dusty town of factories
Stands a house of passing fame,
With a small enchanting garden,
And Polperro is its name.

Here, along the tiny Dutch walls,
Stood stone ornaments in rows.
And in soil behind each statue
Pretty flowers would thrive and grow.

But the statues were the beauty
Of this little garden fair.
There were animals aplenty,
Laughing gnomes were also there.

There were brightly-painted toadstools,
And a sleekly proud black cat,
And a smiling cross-legged pixie
With a sharply-pointed hat.

And a chestnut fawn lay gently
With a sunlight-dappled coat,
And a gaily-coloured parrot
Perched with vivid violet throat.

And a cheeky little puppy,
By a mermaid on a rock
With a gleaming turquoise fishtail
Combing strands of golden locks.

And a chubby owl sat staring
With two dark but friendly eyes,
While a stout yet rigid penguin
Watched each butterfly flit by.

And the owner of this quaint house
Had a young and bright-eyed son
Who would play among the figures
Till the summer's warmth had gone.

For each form meant something special,
Treating each as if alive,
In a garden filled with laughter,
Where delight would always thrive.

And its magic soon attracted
Many other children too –
Gazing round the sunlit pathways,
Where small sparrows often flew.

But one night, when all was sleeping,
Vandals came, and broke each wall,
Stealing many of the figures,
Letting others simply fall

To the ground, to smash and crumble,
Then they left before the dawn.
And at last, when daylight flickered
To create another morn,

Then the owner saw the chaos –
Devastation all around,
Broken walls upon the pathways,
Shattered statues on the ground.

"What has happened to our garden?"
Asked her son with tear-filled eyes,
Far too young and far too honest
To be able to know why

Such a deed as this could happen,
Breaking childhood joys and bliss.
As he saw his owl in pieces,
All that could be said was this:

"In the world in which you're living,
There are people who repel
Everything that isn't evil –
Why this is, no-one can tell.

"But destruction is the only
Way of life that they enjoy.
This is why they broke our garden.
Now you're not a little boy,

"For you've seen the face of envy,
And destruction's savage blow,
And you'll see the like wherever
You may look or you may go.

"For this world is far too bitter,
Far too evil now, it seems,
To allow the never-ending
Of an infant's childhood dreams."

But in time the walls were mended,
And the figures were replaced,
And this garden of enchantment
Still charmed children who had raced

Here to see its sunny statues,
With a parent close behind.
For although in life there's evil,
There is hope as well, we'll find.

Now the boy is grown much older,
Yet his garden will remain,
For the joy it brought to children
Can through all time never wane.

To this boy it was a symbol
Of a true and better world
That one day, from all the darkness
And the woe, would be unfurled.

For although it once was broken,
Still it stands for all to see,
Just as Faith, and Hope, and pure Truth
Last through all Eternity.

The very young puppy in this poem was my first dog, Patch, a rough-haired Jack Russell terrier, who has also appeared, then as a slightly older dog, in a previous poem of mine in Part 4 of this book.

The Puppy

A small, bewhiskered face peers up
Whene'er I call his name,
E'er seeking to attract my gaze
To join him in a game.

A snowy ball of eager fun,
With silky floppy ears,
And deep brown eyes so full of joy
They have no cause for tears.

For like an animated stump
His tail wags fast and few,
As then he waits for my response,
Impatience showing through.

Yet still it wags, with outline blurred,
As each enormous paw
Plods clumsily across the ground
To tap the closing door.

But soon his small bewildered form
Dismisses daylight's charm,
And seeks his box with sleepy eyes
To doze in slumber's calm.

And thus he spends each afternoon,
A tiny ball of white,
Bathed long and deep in Summer's warmth,
And Heaven's golden light.

I wrote this poem in order to show children just how fragile the natural world can be, and in particular to reveal how very vulnerable it is to the destructive, uncaring actions of those humans for whom the wonders and beauty of nature mean nothing. May it be that this poem's message will linger long in the minds of its youthful readers, and as they grow older they will choose to conserve and protect our world rather than to despoil and abuse it.

The Weeping Willow Tree

Every lovely weeping willow
Sadly stands bowed o'er a pool,
Tall and arched in greening beauty,
Stroking waters blue and cool.

For the pretty weeping willow
Cries with leafy tears to see
All the sights that torment Nature,
All the things that shouldn't be.

Here – a pheasant, bright and shining,
Shot in dazzling, whirring flight.
There – a burning match, discarded,
Setting woods and trees alight.

Look – a fox, in breathless panic,
Racing through the fields and hills
Till he drops before the foxhounds,
Who now claim another kill.

See - a mother bird, returning
To her nest now finds it bare,
For her eggs have just been stolen,
By a youth who doesn't care.

E'er the willow sees this sad world,
Filled with woe, and tears, and shame,
Without mercy for the helpless,
Without pity for the lame.

And her grief wells up within her,
Till with tears she bows down low,
And transforms them into dewdrops
Falling to the pool below,

Sparking ripples on the surface,
Sinking deep in waters cool,
As the willow's greening sorrow
Is reflected in the pool.

Weeping willow, lose your sadness,
One fine day you shall not weep.
For the evils people do now,
One dark day these shall they reap.

The power and majesty of the horse has been a source of inspiration for me on many occasions when writing poetry. Consequently, I have attempted to convey these attributes in the following poem penned especially for children, hoping that my words will in at least some small way help to inspire future generations with wonder and respect for this magnificent animal.

White Star

A shining, jet-black horse I see,
A star upon his brow,
So white it glows as bright it grows,
I gaze, and wonder how
A perfect, gleaming star like this
Could be, on such a horse.
So dark is he, as ebony,
A surging equine force

Who gallops o'er the grassy plains,
Or fords the rivers wide.
He leaps and raves in raging waves
Never before defied.
His tail streams in the roaring winds,
His rippling mane flows down.
And o'er his eyes a white star lies,
Just like a silver crown.

White Star, why are you as you are,
So fair in every way?
More than a horse, more like a force
That races through each day –
The symbol of the rugged wild,
Of Nature, true and free.
Ne'er tamed or chained, unspoilt, unstained,
As it was meant to be.

PART 7:
TIME TO SAY GOODBYE…

It is never easy to say goodbye, but down through the ages the poignancy of parting has been expressed and explored in countless poems. So here in this final section, to bid you farewell for now and also to thank you sincerely for taking the time to read what is a very dissimilar book from any that I've previously written, are a few variations of my own on the universal theme of valediction.

When you are old and grey and full of sleep,
And nodding by the fire, take down this book,
And slowly read, and dream of the soft look
Your eyes had once, and of their shadows deep;

How many loved your moments of glad grace,
And loved your beauty with love false or true,
But one man loved the pilgrim soul in you,
And loved the sorrows of your changing face;

And bending down beside the glowing bars,
Murmur, a little sadly, how Love fled
And paced upon the mountains overhead
And hid his face amid a crowd of stars.

W.B. Yeats – 'When You Are Old'

"Goodbye," said the fox.
"And now here is my secret, a very simple secret:
It is only with the heart that one can see rightly; what is essential is invisible to the eye."

Antoine de Saint-Exupéry – *The Little Prince*

Airports so often bring families, friends, and lovers together – but sometimes they can tear them apart.

Airport

A sonic roar, staccato bellow;
A sunlit tear of primrose yellow;
A drift of summer dreaming done.

A world of clouds awaits your calling,
Through which a misty tear is falling –
A silent star of summer gone.

A silver arrow spirals nearer;
My eyes grow dark, and yours are clearer;
For I must stay, and you go on.

And now we part? A moment longer
And then would all my thoughts grow stronger,
And I would be your only one.

But now you leave like evening starlight,
Too soon to be a pale and far light –
Alight where mine has never shone.

And thus a final smile I borrow,
For I shall not see yours tomorrow;
And here, alone, my world has none.

And so goodbye, our dream is over –
A tender, fragile, four-leaved clover
That love I thought for you had won.

But now I see fate's cruel illusion –
There now for us can be no fusion;
God speed your way, the summer's gone.

Age may weaken and ultimately defeat us, the world may change beyond all waking recognition, and the very universe may crumble into nothingness, but love never dies – when all else has vanished, love goes ever on.

And Forever Shall I Wait For You

Though the trees may shrivel and the flowers all die,
Though the moon may vanish far beyond the sky,
Though the stars may shiver in a last goodbye,
I shall wait for you, though my being dies.

As the planets circle in the realms of Space,
And the fire-tipped comets in the twilight race,
I look through the heavens and I see your face,
And I wait for you, though my heart still cries.

I shall wait for you though worlds may come and go,
Though the seas have faltered and may cease to flow,
Though the birds have vanished many years ago,
Still I wait for you, on a bridge of sighs.

And when Darkness comes to fill my final day,
When my soul has wings and softly flies away,
To a Land afar, where every Night is Day,
My soul waits for you, 'cross the endless skies.

Many moons ago, I came upon the name Elvina, which entranced and captivated me, refusing to relinquish my mind from its sweet melancholic enchantment until eventually I penned the following verses, granting it a story and a reality, and in so doing releasing me at last from its haunting charm.

Elvina

When through the violet pool I look,
To see what Fate may show,
Your smiling face still haunts my thoughts
Of worlds from long ago,

When you and I stood here, amidst
Each dappled glade and grove,
And in your hair a small flower shone
Through hazy mists of mauve.

And all around your slender form
The trees in silence stood,
And murmured long your elvish name,
A name so pure and good –

A name as old as Time itself,
Yet bright as sparkling streams.
And in your eyes I saw a world
I visit still in dreams –

A noble world of elvish grace,
Where you no longer are.
And only night birds see my tears
Beneath each silent star,

Like dewdrops on the ruffled grass,
Like pearls upon the flowers,
As I among the woodlands sit
Through many starlit hours,

'Ere morning calls me back once more
To mortal lands and time.
And then I leave this other world
Of memories sublime.

But still I see your smiling face
Within the lucent pool,
And so I stroke its surface bright,
And feel its ripples cool

Embrace my slender fingers 'ere
Your image fades and dies,
To leave me gazing through the blue
Reflection of the skies.

Yet though beyond me you have passed,
From my world you have gone,
With elvish charm, Elvina, still
You are my lovely one.

Endings and beginnings – opposite poles in the spectrum of Time, or different names for one and the same event?

Endings

Such futile things are endings, ne'er
Existing in our world.
For as each moment terminates,
Another is unfurled.

And so all Time turns ever on
Its axis deep in Space.
And ever do the seconds round
In spirals madly race.

For like a book when written, once
The pen is put away
The mind continues writing what
Its thoughts of it portray.

And so the book ne'er ends its tale –
Its end can never be,
As long as all the thoughts it bore
Stretch through Eternity.

And still, undaunted, Time moves on,
Fore'er through Space to wend.
For endings are beginnings, and
Beginnings never end.

Sometimes, not even death is the end...

A Last Visit

High above the greening woodlands,
In the alpine mountainlands,
Sat a tiny village church where
Dappled shadows lay in bands,

Sheltering the humble building
Where I passed one fleeting day,
Up the grassy slopes and hillside
To the clearing where it lay.

And inside, sweet hymns were floating
To the altar and the aisle,
Sung by unseen ghostly voices,
Hymn books rustled for a while,

Yellow pages, worn and battered,
Trembling in the cooling air,
And the stained-glass picture windows
Shone arched rainbows everywhere.

And when all was still and quiet
I moved out, and felt the breeze
Curling round the blooming flowers,
Bustling through the leafy trees.

All lay silent in the churchyard,
Each grave decked with blossoms bright,
And between them grew small snowdrops,
Heads bowed low with petals white.

And at one new grave two snowdrops
Stood and leaned, as if in prayer.
Both so small, but both so splendid,
As their forms shone everywhere.

Here I paused, leaned o'er, and softly
Read the name upon the stone.
Yet I felt no shock or wonder,
For I knew it was my own.

'The Last Spring' is one of Norwegian composer Edvard Grieg's 'Two Elegiac Songs', and listening to the strains of its profoundly sad but hauntingly beautiful melody inspired me to pen the following poem.

The Last Morning

Softly through Space passed the shadow of Morning,
Down through the spirals of starlight and dreams,
Gliding unseen on a shaftlet of primrose,
Dappled with dewdrops and lavender beams,

Softly descending with wings arched and streaming –
Gossamer crescents that soared through the skies,
Sparkling like rainbows as Heaven shone brightly,
Captured by Time in her beautiful eyes.

Yet there lay something that clouded their radiance,
Hiding within them as ever they shone,
And for an instant its shadow engulfed them –
Totally evil, but then it was gone.

She was the Queen of the Dawn and the heavens,
Golden as Light and as endless as Space,
Crowned with a diadem hewn out of amber,
Holding beside her a rose-clustered mace.

Onward she journeyed, through cool shady woodlands,
Lighting their gloom with her soul's golden ray,
Till e'en the trees bowed in silence before her,
Each one entreating their Empress to stay.

For they knew this was her final appearance,
This was her ultimate day upon Earth.
Never again would she come into being,
This time for her there would be no rebirth.

And as she knelt 'neath a bower of green shadows,
Snowy anemones murmured her praise,
While in the distance the clouds hung like phantoms,
Shading the skies in a grey, silent haze.

Then, far away, came a strange, surging rumble,
Choking the world with its venomous breath.
And, as she stood, Morning knew whom it called for,
Cold were its tones, for its image was Death.

Yet from her eyes, veiled by Heaven's blue curtain,
Shining like stars from her beautiful face,
Only a solitary tear trickled slowly,
Downwards to vanish, and leaving no trace.

Now, through the heavens, a spectre rose upwards –
One that her eyes e'er had hidden from view –
Billowing far like a mountain of Evil,
Shrouding the sky with its sickening hue.

And as this hideous wraith filled the heavens,
All of the planet was flooded with tears,
Wept by the mortals who lay in its shadow,
They who created this phantom of Fear.

Gone were the woodlands, each stifled by vapour
Spewed from its lungs as it hovered in Space.
E'en the anemones shrivelled and perished,
Slain by a fiend without flesh, without face.

Yet, neath its cowl – like a shimmering mushroom –
Echoed the grim, eldritch laughter of Doom.
Morning was gone, and anemone petals
Drifted down slowly to cover her tomb.

Does our journey of existence end with the ending of life, or is the ending of life nothing more than a parting from all that has been, with our journey continuing alone, in other forms and along other routes?

The Parting

Like a star in the moonlight,
Like a wave from the shoreline,
All alone with the future,
All the dreaming is done.

Like the birth of a morning,
Now the death of an evening,
For the dawning is over,
And the past has now gone.

Friends and dreams are but shadows
In Oblivion's vortex,
For the show is completed,
And the cast must move on.

Not to look back in silence,
For the past cannot answer,
And a new world is waiting,
Where my heart has not shone.

All my sorrows are ended,
All my joys are departed,
All alone I must travel,
All alone I go on.

What might it be like if we said goodbye to our life not at its end but at its beginning instead, regressing from old age to new birth and the ultimate releasing of our soul? The following, early poem of mine explores this intriguing concept.

Reborn

Borne out of Eternity, back to my home.
I'm eighty-one years old, and live all alone.
Then backwards once more, now my wife at my side,
Down through all the years from the day that I died.

At thirty-five in my young son I take pride,
A small honest boy who has never once lied.
To twenty, to four, and to toys that go 'boom!',
Then back to a foetus in my mother's womb.

The soul of a man who loved all living things –
God sends this pure unborn on fast-flying wings,
To keep up the work of a weary old man,
Who in Heaven lives for the race that he ran.

The rich, evocative Oscar-winning melody written by Francis Lai as the main theme for the movie blockbuster 'Love Story' from 1970 lingered long inside my mind until at last, in sweet supplication, I penned my own lyrics to it, yielding the following poem.

Worlds Apart

Long hours flicker by,
My world still orbits through the shadowed evening sky;
The mournful clouds far past my silhouette still fly,
As I sit thinking of where now my past life lies,
Still ne'er surpassed.

You I e'er recall –
My lifelong dream, consuming being, soul, and all –
You never knew Despair, you never knew a fall
From Fate's fair favour, for you followed e'er her call
To everlast.

For your life was free,
More free, more real than mine could ever hope to be,
A life inspired by Nature's realms eternally,
So that you ceased to notice Mankind's worlds, or me –
Just shadowed casts.

Yes, I always knew,
That I was worlds apart from ever reaching you,
Your world was far beyond mine, sacred, strange, and true;
Yet still in dreams your smiling form comes flooding through –
Now is my Past.

A final word-picture, this time unrhymed, in which I have attempted to recapture via alliteration, onomatopoeia, and selected repetition the subtle beauty and sounds of the seashore experienced one evening alone with only the sands and waves for company, and the thought that perhaps there really is something more out there than merely our own mortality. Until the next time...

Yesterday No Longer – The Seashore By Twilight

Over the slumbering shore I stroll,
over the gently undulating seas of glistening sand,
shining silver in the pale, overlapping light of the moon and stars.

The violet sea flows gently up the silver layers of sandy shore,
coated with white surf, billowing like featherdown.

It makes no sudden, sharp movement as I walk between the grey, red, green, and yellow pebbles strewn over the seashore,
speckled here and there with spiralled shells,
almost as if it too were sleeping,
the mauve and blue waves reflecting silver light that darts back and forth
over their sparkling crests like living shadows cast down from the moon.

As I walk on, the sea stretches alongside, endless in its volume and capacity,
rolling softly over silent shores like a blue fluid wind,
billowing and ruffling,
casting up airborne bubbles to spiral and cycle before bursting,
their souls returning downwards
to be reborn in the waters of the sea.

And as I look at the sea in this dark, silent evening,
it seems as if another world lies beyond its shimmering boundaries,
lying just behind the horizon, to which, one day, we shall all go,
across the rolling waves of the ocean –
leaving behind the silver sands, passing through the tranquil twilight,
until we reach the very end of the ocean itself,
and then at last we shall be there.

We shall have left the world behind,
our cares and our hopes and our dreams all forgotten,
leaving the slumbering sea to caress the sleepy shores forever.

INDEX OF TITLES

Airport	186
And Forever Shall I Wait For You	187
Angel, The	128-32
As Bright as the Waterfall	133
Awakening of Day, The	42
Ballet of the Willows	70-1
Balloon, The	164
Beautiful People, The	16-7
Behold the Thunder Horse	72-4
Bomb, The	75
Borne Into Tomorrow	102-3
Butterfly, The	165
Call From My Past, A	104
Christmas Donkey, The	134-5
Church, The	166
Churchyard, The	166
Clown, The	105
Dandelion Clocks	18
Dismissing Childhood	106
Dragons	96
Dreams of Nature	43-6

Elvina	188-9
Endings	190
Fairy Lullaby	77
Fields of Remembrance	136-7
Fire	19
Fire Pictures	47-8
Fireworks – Bright Flowers of the Night	167
Fly, The	20-1
Flying Horse Fantasia	78-9
Flying Saucer, The	80-1
Forget-Me-Not, The	168
Ghost From The Past, A	107
Ghost, The	49
Green Snake	50
Haunted Cottage, The	82-3
Heaven's Bell	138-40
Here Comes Another Another Rainy Day	141
Last Visit, A	191
Last Morning, The	192-3
Life – The Infinity of the World	142-3
Loch Ness Monster, The	84
Memorial to the Passenger Pigeon, A	22-3
Mirabilis	97
Mirror of Mnemosyne, The	51
Mole, The	169
Mole and the Fieldmouse, The	144-7
Monastery, The	170-1
Monastery Garden, The	148-9
Mother Nature	172
Music of the Spheres, The	150-1
Nightingale, The	24-5
Nod	173
Oberon's Garden	85
Panther, The	97
Papillon	174

Parting, The	194
Patch – A Four-Legged Friend	108-9
Perchance a Mermaid?	86-7
Phantasia of Ghosts and Illusions, A	52-3
Polperro	175-7
Pool of Dreams, The	88-9
Praying Mantis, The	26-7
Puppy, The	178
Reborn	195
Reflections in the Mirror	54
Reflections of Summers Past	110-1
Remembering the Woodlands	112
Robin	113
Robin and the Crossbill, The	152
Rose, The	28
Rose Garden, The	114-5
Scientists, The	116-7
Shadow, The	55
Silence of Solitude, The	118-9
Silver Jubilee Tribute To Her Majesty Queen Elizabeth II, A	120
Sleep	56-7
Snow Dreaming	58-9
Star, The	29
Star Horse, The	90-1
Starlight Fantasia	50-1
Stonehenge	92-3
Sunset, Sunrise	30-1
Swan of Tuonela, The	153
Swans and Horses	32-4
Tattoos	97
Thoughts of a Dreamer	121
Through the Rainbow	35
Tiger, The	36
Transformation of Saint Eustacius, The	154-6
Transforming The Dragon	94
Tribute to Quetzalcoatl, A	95
Unicorn, The	96
Voice of the Winds, The	62-3

Watching the Clouds	37
Weeping Willow Tree, The	179-80
What is God?	157
White Star	181
Wild Roses, The	158
Windmill, The	64
Wonders Untold	159
Worlds Apart	196
Worlds of Faerie	
Yesterday No Longer – The Seashore By Twilight	197
Yesterday's Street	122-3

ACKNOWLEDGEMENTS

First and foremost, I thank with all my heart my family, for their inspiration, guidance, encouragement, and love – without whom and without which I could have accomplished nothing. I only wish that they could all still be here with me today, as they were when I was writing many of the poems in this book, but I draw great comfort from the words of a Hebrew proverb: "Say not in grief: 'They are no more', but live in thankfulness that they were". I do, and shall continue to do so all the days of my life.

I also wish to thank those kind souls down through the years who have read my poetry and commented favourably but fairly upon it, and whose words stayed within my mind until at last they stirred me into preparing this collection for publication. In particular, I am very grateful for the encouraging thoughts of fellow Midlands-based poet Glynnis Briscoe after reading a selection of my poetry many moons ago.

That in turn leads me to thank very sincerely my old friend Jonathan Downes for making this publication happen, and in so doing adding a very different title to the CFZ Press's ever-expanding catalogue of books.

Finally, I wish to thank an old school friend of mine, Nigel Parton, for producing the delightful illustration that appears on this book's front cover, inspiring its title, and which has an interesting little story all of its own.

Entitled 'Star Steed', it is a scraperboard picture that Nigel prepared when we were both around 16 years old. I liked it so much that I purchased it from him for the then-princely sum of £5, and proudly framed it for my bedroom. I also wrote a corresponding poem, 'The Star Horse', inspired by it (and now also included in this book), which I gave to Nigel as an additional payment, ever since when 'Star Steed' has remained framed and on display here at home. I hope that wherever he is today, Nigel has continued his art, and if he has done so, I wonder if he remembers that I was his very first customer?!

ABOUT THE AUTHOR

Born and still living in the West Midlands, England, Dr Karl P.N. Shuker graduated from the University of Leeds with a Bachelor of Science (Honours) degree in pure zoology, and from the University of Birmingham with a Doctor of Philosophy degree in zoology and comparative physiology. He now works full-time as a freelance zoological consultant to the media, and as a prolific published writer.

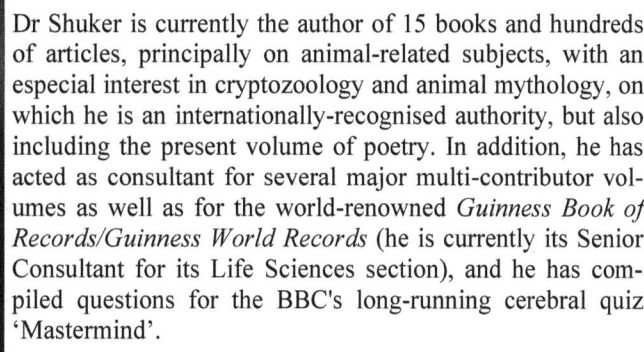

Dr Shuker is currently the author of 15 books and hundreds of articles, principally on animal-related subjects, with an especial interest in cryptozoology and animal mythology, on which he is an internationally-recognised authority, but also including the present volume of poetry. In addition, he has acted as consultant for several major multi-contributor volumes as well as for the world-renowned *Guinness Book of Records/Guinness World Records* (he is currently its Senior Consultant for its Life Sciences section), and he has compiled questions for the BBC's long-running cerebral quiz 'Mastermind'.

Dr Shuker has travelled the world in the course of his researches and writings, and has appeared regularly on television and radio. Aside from work, his diverse range of interests include motorbikes, the life and career of James Dean, collecting masquerade and carnival masks, quizzes, philately, poetry, travel, world mythology, and the history of animation.

He is a Scientific Fellow of the prestigious Zoological Society of London, a Fellow of the Royal Entomological Society, and a member of several other wildlife-related organisations, he is Cryptozoology Consultant and West Midlands Representative to the Centre for Fortean Zoology, and is also a Member of the Society of Authors.

Dr Shuker's personal website can be accessed at http://www.karlshuker.com, and his blog, ShukerNature, can be accessed at http://www.karlshuker.blogspot.com. There is also an entry for Dr Shuker in the online encyclopedia Wikipedia, and a fan page on Facebook.

AUTHOR BIBLIOGRAPHY

Mystery Cats of the World: From Blue Tigers To Exmoor Beasts (Robert Hale: London, 1989)
Extraordinary Animals Worldwide (Robert Hale: London, 1991)
The Lost Ark: New and Rediscovered Animals of the 20th Century (HarperCollins: London, 1993)
Dragons: A Natural History (Aurum: London/Simon & Schuster: New York, 1995; republished Taschen: Cologne, 2006)
In Search of Prehistoric Survivors: Do Giant 'Extinct' Creatures Still Exist? (Blandford: London, 1995)
The Unexplained: An Illustrated Guide to the World's Natural and Paranormal Mysteries (Carlton: London/JG Press: North Dighton, 1996; republished Carlton: London, 2002)
From Flying Toads To Snakes With Wings: From the Pages of FATE Magazine (Llewellyn: St Paul, 1997; republished Bounty: London, 2005)
Mysteries of Planet Earth: An Encyclopedia of the Inexplicable (Carlton: London, 1999)
The Hidden Powers of Animals: Uncovering the Secrets of Nature (Reader's Digest: Pleasantville/Marshall Editions: London, 2001)
The New Zoo: New and Rediscovered Animals of the Twentieth Century [fully-updated, greatly-expanded, new edition of *The Lost Ark*] (House of Stratus Ltd: Thirsk, UK/House of Stratus Inc: Poughkeepsie, USA, 2002)
The Beasts That Hide From Man: Seeking the World's Last Undiscovered Animals (Paraview: New York, 2003)
Extraordinary Animals Revisited: From Singing Dogs To Serpent Kings (CFZ Press: Bideford, 2007)
Dr Shuker's Casebook: In Pursuit of Marvels and Mysteries (CFZ Press: Bideford, 2008)
Dinosaurs and Other Prehistoric Animals on Stamps: A Worldwide Catalogue (CFZ Press: Bideford, 2008).
Star Steeds and Other Dreams: The Collected Poems (CFZ Press: Bideford, 2009).

Consultant and also Contributor
Man and Beast (Reader's Digest: Pleasantville, New York, 1993)
Secrets of the Natural World (Reader's Digest: Pleasantville, New York, 1993)
Almanac of the Uncanny (Reader's Digest: Surry Hills, Australia, 1995)
The Guinness Book of Records/Guinness World Records 1998-present day (Guinness: London, 1997-present day)

Consultant
Monsters (Lorenz: London, 2001)

Contributor
Of Monsters and Miracles CD-ROM (Croydon Museum/Interactive Designs: Oxton, 1995)
Fortean Times Weird Year 1996 (John Brown Publishing: London, 1996)
Mysteries of the Deep (Llewellyn: St Paul, 1998)
Guinness Amazing Future (Guinness: London, 1999)
The Earth (Channel 4 Books: London, 2000)
Mysteries and Monsters of the Sea (Gramercy: New York, 2001)
Chambers Dictionary of the Unexplained (Chambers: Edinburgh, 2007)
Chambers Myths and Mysteries (Chambers: Edinburgh, 2008)
The Fortean Times Paranormal Handbook (Dennis Publishing: London, 2009)
Plus numerous contributions to the annual *CFZ Yearbook* series of volumes

THE CENTRE FOR FORTEAN ZOOLOGY

So, what is the Centre for Fortean Zoology?

We are a non profit-making organisation founded in 1992 with the aim of being a clearing house for information, and coordinating research into mystery animals around the world. We also study out of place animals, rare and aberrant animal behaviour, and Zooform Phenomena; little-understood "things" that appear to be animals, but which are in fact nothing of the sort, and not even alive (at least in the way we understand the term).

Why should I join the Centre for Fortean Zoology?

Not only are we the biggest organisation of our type in the world, but - or so we like to think - we are the best. We are certainly the only truly global Cryptozoological research organisation, and we carry out our investigations using a strictly scientific set of guidelines. We are expanding all the time and looking to recruit new members to help us in our research into mysterious animals and strange creatures across the globe. Why should you join us? Because, if you are genuinely interested in trying to solve the last great mysteries of Mother Nature, there is nobody better than us with whom to do it.

What do I get if I join the Centre for Fortean Zoology?

For £12 a year, you get a four-issue subscription to our journal *Animals & Men*. Each issue contains 60 pages packed with news, articles, letters, research papers, field reports, and even a gossip column! The magazine is A5 in format with a full colour cover. You also have access to one of the world's largest collections of resource material dealing with cryptozoology and allied disciplines, and people from the CFZ membership regularly take part in fieldwork and expeditions around the world.

How is the Centre for Fortean Zoology organized?

The CFZ is managed by a three-man board of trustees, with a non-profit making trust registered with HM Government Stamp Office. The board of trustees is supported by a Permanent Directorate of full and part-time staff, and advised by a Consultancy Board of specialists - many of whom are world-renowned experts in their particular field. We have regional representatives across the UK, the USA, and many other parts of the world, and are affiliated with other organisations whose aims and protocols mirror our own.

I am new to the subject, and although I am interested I have little practical knowledge. I don't want to feel out of my depth. What should I do?

Don't worry. We were *all* beginners once. You'll find that the people at the CFZ are friendly and approachable. We have a thriving forum on the website which is the hub of an ever-growing electronic community. You will soon find your feet. Many members of the CFZ Permanent Directorate started off as ordinary members, and now work full-time chasing monsters around the world.

I have an idea for a project which isn't on your website. What do I do?

Write to us, e-mail us, or telephone us. The list of future projects on the website is not exhaustive. If you have a good idea for an investigation, please tell us. We may well be able to help.

How do I go on an expedition?

We are always looking for volunteers to join us. If you see a project that interests you, do not hesitate to get in touch with us. Under certain circumstances we can help provide funding for your trip. If you look on the future projects section of the website, you can see some of the projects that we have pencilled in for the next few years.

In 2003 and 2004 we sent three-man expeditions to Sumatra looking for Orang-Pendek - a semi-legendary bipedal ape. The same three went to Mongolia in 2005. All three members started off merely subscribers to the CFZ magazine.

Next time it could be you!

Project Kerinci, Sumatra - 2003
In search of the bipedal ape Orang Pendek

How is the Centre for Fortean Zoology funded?

We have no magic sources of income. All our funds come from donations, membership fees, works that we do for TV, radio or magazines, and sales of our publications and merchandise. We are always looking for corporate sponsorship, and other sources of revenue. If you have any ideas for fund-raising please let us know. However, unlike other cryptozoological organisations in the past, we do not live in an intellectual ivory tower. We are not afraid to get our hands dirty, and furthermore we are not one of those organisations where the membership have to raise money so that a privileged few can go on expensive foreign trips. Our research teams, both in the UK and abroad, consist of a mixture of experienced and inexperienced personnel. We are truly a community, and work on the premise that the benefits of CFZ membership are open to all.

What do you do with the data you gather from your investigations and expeditions?

Reports of our investigations are published on our website as soon as they are available. Preliminary reports are posted within days of the project finishing.

Each year we publish a 200 page yearbook containing research papers and expedition reports too long to be printed in the journal. We freely circulate our information to anybody who asks for it.

Is the CFZ community purely an electronic one?

No. Each year since 2000 we have held our annual convention - the *Weird Weekend* - in Exeter. It is three days of lectures, workshops, and excursions. But most importantly it is a chance for members of the CFZ to meet each other, and to talk with the members of the permanent directorate in a relaxed and informal setting and preferably with a pint of beer in one hand. Since 2006 - the *Weird Weekend* has been bigger and better and held on the third weekend in August in the idyllic rural location of Woolsery in North Devon.

Since relocating to North Devon in 2005 we have become ever more closely involved with other community organisations, and we hope that this trend will continue. We also work closely with Police Forces across the UK as consultants for animal mutilation cases, and we intend to forge closer links with the coastguard and other community services. We want to work closely with those who regularly travel into the Bristol Channel, so that if the recent trend of exotic animal visitors to our coastal waters continues, we can be out there as soon as possible.

We are building a Visitor's Centre in rural North Devon. This will not be open to the general public, but will provide a museum, a library and an educational resource for our members (currently over 400) across the globe. We are also planning a youth organisation which will involve children and young people in our activities.

Apart from having been the only Fortean Zoological organisation in the world to have consistently published material on all aspects of the subject for over a decade, we have achieved the following concrete results:

- Disproved the myth relating to the headless so-called sea-serpent carcass of Durgan beach in Cornwall 1975
- Disproved the story of the 1988 puma skull of Lustleigh Cleave
- Carried out the only in-depth research ever into the mythos of the Cornish Owlman
- Made the first records of a tropical species of lamprey
- Made the first records of a luminous cave gnat larva in Thailand
- Discovered a possible new species of British mammal - the beech marten
- In 1994-6 carried out the first archival fortean zoological survey of Hong Kong
- In the year 2000, CFZ theories were confirmed when an new species of lizard was added to the British list
- Identified the monster of Martin Mere in Lancashire as a giant wels catfish
- Expanded the known range of Armitage's skink in the Gambia by 80%
- Obtained photographic evidence of the remains of Europe's largest known pike
- Carried out the first ever in-depth study of the *ninki-nanka*
- Carried out the first attempt to breed Puerto Rican cave snails in captivity
- Were the first European explorers to visit the `lost valley` in Sumatra
- Published the first ever evidence for a new tribe of pygmies in Guyana
- Published the first evidence for a new species of caiman in Guyana
- Filmed unknown creatures on a monster-haunted lake in Ireland for the first time
- Had a sighting of orang pendek in Sumatra in 2009
- Published some of the best evidence ever for the almasty in southern Russia

EXPEDITIONS & INVESTIGATIONS TO DATE INCLUDE:

- 1998 Puerto Rico, Florida, Mexico *(Chupacabras)*
- 1999 Nevada *(Bigfoot)*
- 2000 Thailand *(Giant snakes called nagas)*
- 2002 Martin Mere *(Giant catfish)*
- 2002 Cleveland *(Wallaby mutilation)*
- 2003 Bolam Lake *(BHM Reports)*
- 2003 Sumatra *(Orang Pendek)*
- 2003 Texas *(Bigfoot; giant snapping turtles)*
- 2004 Sumatra *(Orang Pendek; cigau, a sabre-toothed cat)*
- 2004 Illinois *(Black panthers; cicada swarm)*
- 2004 Texas *(Mystery blue dog)*
- Loch Morar *(Monster)*
- 2004 Puerto Rico *(Chupacabras; carnivorous cave snails)*
- 2005 Belize *(Affiliate expedition for hairy dwarfs)*
- 2005 Loch Ness *(Monster)*
- 2005 Mongolia *(Allghoi Khorkhoi aka Mongolian death worm)*
- 2006 Gambia *(Gambo - Gambian sea monster , Ninki Nanka and Armitage's skink*
- 2006 Llangorse Lake *(Giant pike, giant eels)*
- 2006 Windermere *(Giant eels)*
- 2007 Coniston Water *(Giant eels)*
- 2007 Guyana *(Giant anaconda, didi, water tiger)*
- 2008 Russia *(Almasty)*
- 2009 Sumatra *(Orang pendek)*
- 2009 Republic of Ireland *(Lake Monster)*

Other books available from
CFZ PRESS

THE OWLMAN AND OTHERS - 30th Anniversary Edition
Jonathan Downes - ISBN 978-1-905723-02-7   £14.99

EASTER 1976 - Two young girls playing in the churchyard of Mawnan Old Church in southern Cornwall were frightened by what they described as a "nasty bird-man". A series of sightings that has continued to the present day. These grotesque and frightening episodes have fascinated researchers for three decades now, and one man has spent years collecting all the available evidence into a book. To mark the 30th anniversary of these sightings, Jonathan Downes has published a special edition of his book.

DRAGONS - More than a myth?
Richard Freeman - ISBN 0-9512872-9-X   £14.99

First scientific look at dragons since 1884. It looks at dragon legends worldwide, and examines modern sightings of dragon-like creatures, as well as some of the more esoteric theories surrounding dragonkind.

Dragons are discussed from a folkloric, historical and cryptozoological perspective, and Richard Freeman concludes that: "When your parents told you that dragons don't exist - they lied!"

MONSTER HUNTER
Jonathan Downes - ISBN 0-9512872-7-3   £14.99

Jonathan Downes' long-awaited autobiography, *Monster Hunter*...

Written with refreshing candour, it is the extraordinary story of an extraordinary life, in which the author crosses paths with wizards, rock stars, terrorists, and a bewildering array of mythical and not so mythical monsters, and still just about manages to emerge with his sanity intact.......

MONSTER OF THE MERE
Jonathan Downes - ISBN 0-9512872-2-2   £12.50

It all starts on Valentine's Day 2002 when a Lancashire newspaper announces that "Something" has been attacking swans at a nature reserve in Lancashire. Eyewitnesses have reported that a giant unknown creature has been dragging fully grown swans beneath the water at Martin Mere. An intrepid team from the Exeter based Centre for Fortean Zoology, led by the author, make two trips – each of a week – to the lake and its surrounding marshlands. During their investigations they uncover a thrilling and complex web of historical fact and fancy, quasi Fortean occurrences, strange animals and even human sacrifice.

**CFZ PRESS, MYRTLE COTTAGE,
WOOLFARDISWORTHY BIDEFORD,
NORTH DEVON, EX39 5QR
www.cfz.org.uk**

Other books available from
CFZ PRESS

CFZ PRESS

ONLY FOOLS AND GOATSUCKERS
Jonathan Downes - ISBN 0-9512872-3-0

£12.50

In January and February 1998 Jonathan Downes and Graham Inglis of the Centre for Fortean Zoology spent three and a half weeks in Puerto Rico, Mexico and Florida, accompanied by a film crew from UK Channel 4 TV. Their aim was to make a documentary about the terrifying chupacabra - a vampiric creature that exists somewhere in the grey area between folklore and reality. This remarkable book tells the gripping, sometimes scary, and often hilariously funny story of how the boys from the CFZ did their best to subvert the medium of contemporary TV documentary making and actually do their job.

WHILE THE CAT'S AWAY
Chris Moiser - ISBN: 0-9512872-1-4

£7.99

Over the past thirty years or so there have been numerous sightings of large exotic cats, including black leopards, pumas and lynx, in the South West of England. Former Rhodesian soldier Sam McCall moved to North Devon and became a farmer and pub owner when Rhodesia became Zimbabwe in 1980. Over the years despite many of his pub regulars having seen the "Beast of Exmoor" Sam wasn't at all sure that it existed. Then a series of happenings made him change his mind. Chris Moiser—a zoologist—is well known for his research into the mystery cats of the westcountry. This is his first novel.

CFZ EXPEDITION REPORT 2006 - GAMBIA
ISBN 1905723032

£12.50

In July 2006, The J.T.Downes memorial Gambia Expedition - a six-person team - Chris Moiser, Richard Freeman, Chris Clarke, Oll Lewis, Lisa Dowley and Suzi Marsh went to the Gambia, West Africa. They went in search of a dragon-like creature, known to the natives as `Ninki Nanka`, which has terrorized the tiny African state for generations, and has reportedly killed people as recently as the 1990s. They also went to dig up part of a beach where an amateur naturalist claims to have buried the carcass of a mysterious fifteen foot sea monster named 'Gambo', and they sought to find the Armitage's Skink (*Chalcides armitagei*) - a tiny lizard first described in 1922 and only rediscovered in 1989. Here, for the first time, is their story.... With an forward by Dr. Karl Shuker and introduction by Jonathan Downes.

BIG CATS IN BRITAIN YEARBOOK 2006
Edited by Mark Fraser - ISBN 978-1905723-01-0

£10.00

Big cats are said to roam the British Isles and Ireland even now as you are sitting and reading this. People from all walks of life encounter these mysterious felines on a daily basis in every nook and cranny of these two countries. Most are jet-black, some are white, some are brown, in fact big cats of every description and colour are seen by some unsuspecting person while on his or her daily business. 'Big Cats in Britain' are the largest and most active group in the British Isles and Ireland This is their first book. It contains a run-down of every known big cat sighting in the UK during 2005, together with essays by various luminaries of the British big cat research community which place the phenomenon into scientific, cultural, and historical perspective.

**CFZ PRESS, MYRTLE COTTAGE,
WOOLSERY, BIDEFORD,
NORTH DEVON, EX39 5QR
w w w . c f z . o r g . u k**

Other books available from
CFZ PRESS

THE SMALLER MYSTERY CARNIVORES OF THE WESTCOUNTRY
Jonathan Downes - ISBN 978-1-905723-05-8

£7.99

Although much has been written in recent years about the mystery big cats which have been reported stalking Westcountry moorlands, little has been written on the subject of the smaller British mystery carnivores. This unique book redresses the balance and examines the current status in the Westcountry of three species thought to be extinct: the Wildcat, the Pine Marten and the Polecat, finding that the truth is far more exciting than the currently held scientific dogma. This book also uncovers evidence suggesting that even more exotic species of small mammal may lurk hitherto unsuspected in the countryside of Devon, Cornwall, Somerset and Dorset.

THE BLACKDOWN MYSTERY
Jonathan Downes - ISBN 978-1-905723-00-3

£7.99

Intrepid members of the CFZ are up to the challenge, and manage to entangle themselves thoroughly in the bizarre trappings of this case. This is the soft underbelly of ufology, rife with unsavoury characters, plenty of drugs and booze." That sums it up quite well, we think. A new edition of the classic 1999 book by legendary fortean author Jonathan Downes. In this remarkable book, Jon weaves a complex tale of conspiracy, anti-conspiracy, quasi-conspiracy and downright lies surrounding an air-crash and alleged UFO incident in Somerset during 1996. However the story is much stranger than that. This excellent and amusing book lifts the lid off much of contemporary forteana and explains far more than it initially promises.

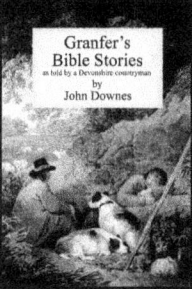

GRANFER'S BIBLE STORIES
John Downes - ISBN 0-9512872-8-1

£7.99

Bible stories in the Devonshire vernacular, each story being told by an old Devon Grandfather - 'Granfer'. These stories are now collected together in a remarkable book presenting selected parts of the Bible as one more-or-less continuous tale in short 'bite sized' stories intended for dipping into or even for bed-time reading. `Granfer` treats the biblical characters as if they were simple country folk living in the next village. Many of the stories are treated with a degree of bucolic humour and kindly irreverence, which not only gives the reader an opportunity to re-evaluate familiar tales in a new light, but do so in both an entertaining and a spiritually uplifting manner.

FRAGRANT HARBOURS DISTANT RIVERS
John Downes - ISBN 0-9512872-5-7

£12.50

Many excellent books have been written about Africa during the second half of the 19th Century, but this one is unique in that it presents the stories of a dozen different people, whose interlinked lives and achievements have as many nuances as any contemporary soap opera. It explains how the events in China and Hong Kong which surrounded the Opium Wars, intimately effected the events in Africa which take up the majority of this book. The author served in the Colonial Service in Nigeria and Hong Kong, during which he found himself following in the footsteps of one of the main characters in this book; Frederick Lugard – the architect of modern Nigeria.

**CFZ PRESS, MYRTLE COTTAGE,
WOOLFARDISWORTHY BIDEFORD,
NORTH DEVON, EX39 5QR
w w w . c f z . o r g . u k**

Other books available from
CFZ PRESS

ANIMALS & MEN - Issues 1 - 5 - In the Beginning
Edited by Jonathan Downes - ISBN 0-9512872-6-5

£12.50

At the beginning of the 21st Century monsters still roam the remote, and sometimes not so remote, corners of our planet. It is our job to search for them. The Centre for Fortean Zoology [CFZ] is the only professional, scientific and full-time organisation in the world dedicated to cryptozoology - the study of unknown animals. Since 1992 the CFZ has carried out an unparalleled programme of research and investigation all over the world. We have carried out expeditions to Sumatra (2003 and 2004), Mongolia (2005), Puerto Rico (1998 and 2004), Mexico (1998), Thailand (2000), Florida (1998), Nevada (1999 and 2003), Texas (2003 and 2004), and Illinois (2004). An introductory essay by Jonathan Downes, notes putting each issue into a historical perspective, and a history of the CFZ.

ANIMALS & MEN - Issues 6 - 10 - The Number of the Beast
Edited by Jonathan Downes - ISBN 978-1-905723-06-5

£12.50

At the beginning of the 21st Century monsters still roam the remote, and sometimes not so remote, corners of our planet. It is our job to search for them. The Centre for Fortean Zoology [CFZ] is the only professional, scientific and full-time organisation in the world dedicated to cryptozoology - the study of unknown animals. Since 1992 the CFZ has carried out an unparalleled programme of research and investigation all over the world. We have carried out expeditions to Sumatra (2003 and 2004), Mongolia (2005), Puerto Rico (1998 and 2004), Mexico (1998), Thailand (2000), Florida (1998), Nevada (1999 and 2003), Texas (2003 and 2004), and Illinois (2004). Preface by Mark North and an introductory essay by Jonathan Downes, notes putting each issue into a historical perspective, and a history of the CFZ.

BIG BIRD! Modern Sightings of Flying Monsters

Ken Gerhard - ISBN 978-1-905723-08-9

£7.99

From all over the dusty U.S./Mexican border come hair-raising stories of modern day encounters with winged monsters of immense size and terrifying appearance. Further field sightings of similar creatures are recorded from all around the globe. What lies behind these weird tales? Ken Gerhard is a native Texan, he lives in the homeland of the monster some call 'Big Bird'. Ken's scholarly work is the first of its kind. On the track of the monster, Ken uncovers cases of animal mutilations, attacks on humans and mounting evidence of a stunning zoological discovery ignored by mainstream science. Keep watching the skies!

STRENGTH THROUGH KOI
They saved Hitler's Koi and other stories

Jonathan Downes - **ISBN** 978-1-905723-04-1

£7.99

Strength through Koi is a book of short stories - some of them true, some of them less so - by noted cryptozoologist and raconteur Jonathan Downes. The stories are all about koi carp, and their interaction with bigfoot, UFOs, and Nazis. Even the late George Harrison makes an appearance. Very funny in parts, this book is highly recommended for anyone with even a passing interest in aquaculture, but should be taken definitely *cum grano salis*.

CFZ PRESS, MYRTLE COTTAGE, WOOLSERY, BIDEFORD, NORTH DEVON, EX39 5QR

Other books available from
CFZ PRESS

BIG CATS IN BRITAIN YEARBOOK 2007
Edited by Mark Fraser - ISBN 978-1-905723-09-6

£12.50

People from all walks of life encounter mysterious felids on a daily basis, in every nook and cranny of the UK. Most are jet-black, some are white, some are brown; big cats of every description and colour are seen by some unsuspecting person while on his or her daily business. 'Big Cats in Britain' are the largest and most active research group in the British Isles and Ireland. This book contains a run-down of every known big cat sighting in the UK during 2006, together with essays by various luminaries of the British big cat research community.

CAT FLAPS! Northern Mystery Cats
Andy Roberts - ISBN 978-1-905723-11-9

£6.99

Of all Britain's mystery beasts, the alien big cats are the most renowned. In recent years the notoriety of these uncatchable, out-of-place predators have eclipsed even the Loch Ness Monster. They slink from the shadows to terrorise a community, and then, as often as not, vanish like ghosts. But now film, photographs, livestock kills, and paw prints show that we can no longer deny the existence of these once-legendary beasts. Here then is a case-study, a true lost classic of Fortean research by one of the country's most respected researchers.

CENTRE FOR FORTEAN ZOOLOGY 2007 YEARBOOK
Edited by Jonathan Downes and Richard Freeman
ISBN 978-1-905723-14-0

£12.50

The Centre For Fortean Zoology Yearbook is a collection of papers and essays too long and detailed for publication in the CFZ Journal *Animals & Men*. With contributions from both well-known researchers, and relative newcomers to the field, the Yearbook provides a forum where new theories can be expounded, and work on little-known cryptids discussed.

MONSTER! THE A-Z OF ZOOFORM PHENOMENA
Neil Arnold - ISBN 978-1-905723-10-2

£14.99

Zooform Phenomena are the most elusive, and least understood, mystery `animals`. Indeed, they are not animals at all, and are not even animate in the accepted terms of the word. Author and researcher Neil Arnold is to be commended for a groundbreaking piece of work, and has provided the world's first alphabetical listing of zooforms from around the world.

**CFZ PRESS, MYRTLE COTTAGE,
WOOLFARDISWORTHY BIDEFORD,
NORTH DEVON, EX39 5QR
www.cfz.org.uk**

Other books available from
CFZ PRESS

BIG CATS LOOSE IN BRITAIN
Marcus Matthews - ISBN 978-1-905723-12-6

£14.99

Big Cats: Loose in Britain, looks at the body of anecdotal evidence for such creatures: sightings, livestock kills, paw-prints and photographs, and seeks to determine underlying commonalities and threads of evidence. These two strands are repeatedly woven together into a highly readable, yet scientifically compelling, overview of the big cat phenomenon in Britain.

DARK DORSET
TALES OF MYSTERY, WONDER AND TERROR
Robert. J. Newland and Mark. J. North
ISBN 978-1-905723-15-6

£12.50

This extensively illustrated compendium has over 400 tales and references, making this book by far one of the best in its field. Dark Dorset has been thoroughly researched, and includes many new entries and up to date information never before published. The title of the book speaks for itself, and is indeed not for the faint hearted or those easily shocked.

MAN-MONKEY - IN SEARCH OF THE BRITISH BIGFOOT
Nick Redfern - ISBN 978-1-905723-16-4

£9.99

In her 1883 book, *Shropshire Folklore*, Charlotte S. Burne wrote: *'Just before he reached the canal bridge, a strange black creature with great white eyes sprang out of the plantation by the roadside and alighted on his horse's back'*. The creature duly became known as the `Man-Monkey`.

Between 1986 and early 2001, Nick Redfern delved deeply into the mystery of the strange creature of that dark stretch of canal. Now, published for the very first time, are Nick's original interview notes, his files and discoveries; as well as his theories pertaining to what lies at the heart of this diabolical legend.

EXTRAORDINARY ANIMALS REVISITED
Dr Karl Shuker - ISBN 978-1905723171

£14.99

This delightful book is the long-awaited, greatly-expanded new edition of one of Dr Karl Shuker's much-loved early volumes, *Extraordinary Animals Worldwide*. It is a fascinating celebration of what used to be called romantic natural history, examining a dazzling diversity of animal anomalies, creatures of cryptozoology, and all manner of other thought-provoking zoological revelations and continuing controversies down through the ages of wildlife discovery.

CFZ PRESS, MYRTLE COTTAGE,
WOOLFARDISWORTHY BIDEFORD,
NORTH DEVON, EX39 5QR
w w w . c f z . o r g . u k

Other books available from
CFZ PRESS

DARK DORSET CALENDAR CUSTOMS
Robert J Newland - ISBN 978-1-905723-18-8

£12.50

Much of the intrinsic charm of Dorset folklore is owed to the importance of folk customs. Today only a small amount of these curious and occasionally eccentric customs have survived, while those that still continue have, for many of us, lost their original significance. Why do we eat pancakes on Shrove Tuesday? Why do children dance around the maypole on May Day? Why do we carve pumpkin lanterns at Hallowe'en? All the answers are here! Robert has made an in-depth study of the Dorset country calendar identifying the major feast-days, holidays and celebrations when traditionally such folk customs are practiced.

CENTRE FOR FORTEAN ZOOLOGY 2004 YEARBOOK
Edited by Jonathan Downes and Richard Freeman
ISBN 978-1-905723-14-0

£12.50

The Centre For Fortean Zoology Yearbook is a collection of papers and essays too long and detailed for publication in the CFZ Journal *Animals & Men*. With contributions from both well-known researchers, and relative newcomers to the field, the Yearbook provides a forum where new theories can be expounded, and work on little-known cryptids discussed.

CENTRE FOR FORTEAN ZOOLOGY 2008 YEARBOOK
Edited by Jonathan Downes and Corinna Downes
ISBN 978 -1-905723-19-5

£12.50

The Centre For Fortean Zoology Yearbook is a collection of papers and essays too long and detailed for publication in the CFZ Journal *Animals & Men*. With contributions from both well-known researchers, and relative newcomers to the field, the Yearbook provides a forum where new theories can be expounded, and work on little-known cryptids discussed.

ETHNA'S JOURNAL
Corinna Newton Downes
ISBN 978 -1-905723-21-8

£9.99

Ethna's Journal tells the story of a few months in an alternate Dark Ages, seen through the eyes of Ethna, daughter of Lord Edric. She is an unsophisticated girl from the fortress town of Cragnuth, somewhere in the north of England, who reluctantly gets embroiled in a web of treachery, sorcery and bloody war...

**CFZ PRESS, MYRTLE COTTAGE,
WOOLFARDISWORTHY BIDEFORD,
NORTH DEVON, EX39 5QR
www.cfz.org.uk**

Other books available from
CFZ PRESS

ANIMALS & MEN - Issues 11 - 15 - The Call of the Wild
Jonathan Downes (Ed) - ISBN 978-1-905723-07-2

£12.50

Since 1994 we have been publishing the world's only dedicated cryptozoology magazine, *Animals & Men*. This volume contains fascimile reprints of issues 11 to 15 and includes articles covering out of place walruses, feathered dinosaurs, possible North American ground sloth survival, the theory of initial bipedalism, mystery whales, mitten crabs in Britain, Barbary lions, out of place animals in Germany, mystery pangolins, the barking beast of Bath, Yorkshire ABCs, Molly the singing oyster, singing mice, the dragons of Yorkshire, singing mice, the bigfoot murders, waspman, British beavers, the migo, Nessie, the weird warbling whatsit of the westcountry, the quagga project and much more...

IN THE WAKE OF BERNARD HEUVELMANS
Michael A Woodley - ISBN 978-1-905723-20-1

£9.99

Everyone is familiar with the nautical maps from the middle ages that were liberally festooned with images of exotic and monstrous animals, but the truth of the matter is that the *idea* of the sea monster is probably as old as humankind itself.

For two hundred years, scientists have been producing speculative classifications of sea serpents, attempting to place them within a zoological framework. This book looks at these successive classification models, and using a new formula produces a sea serpent classification for the 21st Century.

CENTRE FOR FORTEAN ZOOLOGY 1999 YEARBOOK
Edited by Jonathan Downes
ISBN 978 -1-905723-24-9

£12.50

The Centre For Fortean Zoology Yearbook is a collection of papers and essays too long and detailed for publication in the CFZ Journal *Animals & Men*. With contributions from both well-known researchers, and relative newcomers to the field, the Yearbook provides a forum where new theories can be expounded, and work on little-known cryptids discussed.

CENTRE FOR FORTEAN ZOOLOGY 1996 YEARBOOK
Edited by Jonathan Downes
ISBN 978 -1-905723-22-5

£12.50

The Centre For Fortean Zoology Yearbook is a collection of papers and essays too long and detailed for publication in the CFZ Journal *Animals & Men*. With contributions from both well-known researchers, and relative newcomers to the field, the Yearbook provides a forum where new theories can be expounded, and work on little-known cryptids discussed.

CFZ PRESS, MYRTLE COTTAGE, WOOLFARDISWORTHY BIDEFORD, NORTH DEVON, EX39 5QR
w w w . c f z . o r g . u k

Other books available from
CFZ PRESS

BIG CATS IN BRITAIN YEARBOOK 2008
Edited by Mark Fraser - ISBN 978-1-905723-23-2

£12.50

People from all walks of life encounter mysterious felids on a daily basis, in every nook and cranny of the UK. Most are jet-black, some are white, some are brown; big cats of every description and colour are seen by some unsuspecting person while on his or her daily business. 'Big Cats in Britain' are the largest and most active research group in the British Isles and Ireland. This book contains a run-down of every known big cat sighting in the UK during 2007, together with essays by various luminaries of the British big cat research community.

CFZ EXPEDITION REPORT 2007 - GUYANA
ISBN 978-1-905723-25-6

£12.50

Since 1992, the CFZ has carried out an unparalleled programme of research and investigation all over the world. In November 2007, a five-person team - Richard Freeman, Chris Clarke, Paul Rose, Lisa Dowley and Jon Hare went to Guyana, South America. They went in search of giant anacondas, the bigfoot-like didi, and the terrifying water tiger.

Here, for the first time, is their story...With an introduction by Jonathan Downes and forward by Dr. Karl Shuker.

CENTRE FOR FORTEAN ZOOLOGY 2003 YEARBOOK
Edited by Jonathan Downes and Richard Freeman
ISBN 978 -1-905723-19-5

£12.50

The Centre For Fortean Zoology Yearbook is a collection of papers and essays too long and detailed for publication in the CFZ Journal *Animals & Men*. With contributions from both well-known researchers, and relative newcomers to the field, the Yearbook provides a forum where new theories can be expounded, and work on little-known cryptids discussed.

CENTRE FOR FORTEAN ZOOLOGY 1997 YEARBOOK
Edited by Jonathan Downes and Graham Inglis
ISBN 978 -1-905723-27-0

£12.50

The Centre For Fortean Zoology Yearbook is a collection of papers and essays too long and detailed for publication in the CFZ Journal *Animals & Men*. With contributions from both well-known researchers, and relative newcomers to the field, the Yearbook provides a forum where new theories can be expounded, and work on little-known cryptids discussed.

**CFZ PRESS, MYRTLE COTTAGE,
WOOLFARDISWORTHY BIDEFORD,
NORTH DEVON, EX39 5QR
w w w . c f z . o r g . u k**

Other books available from
CFZ PRESS

CENTRE FOR FORTEAN ZOOLOGY 2000-1 YEARBOOK
Edited by Jonathan Downes and Richard Freeman
ISBN 978-1-905723-19-5

£12.50

The Centre For Fortean Zoology Yearbook is a collection of papers and essays too long and detailed for publication in the CFZ Journal *Animals & Men*. With contributions from both well-known researchers, and relative newcomers to the field, the Yearbook provides a forum where new theories can be expounded, and work on little-known cryptids discussed.

THE MYSTERY ANIMALS OF THE BRITISH ISLES: NORTHUMBERLAND AND TYNESIDE
Michael J Hallowell
ISBN 978-1-905723-29-4

£12.50

Mystery animals? Great Britain? Surely not. But is is true.

This is a major new series from CFZ Press. It will cover Great Britain and the Republic of Ireland, on a county by county basis, describing the mystery animals of the entire island group.

The Island of Paradise: Chupacabra, UFO Crash Retrievals, and Accelerated Evolution on the Island of Puerto Rico
Jonathan Downes - ISBN 978-1-905723-32-4

£14.99

In his first book of original research for four years, Jon Downes visits the Antillean island of Puerto Rico, to which he has led two expeditions - in 1998 and 2004. Together with noted researcher Nick Redfern he goes in search of the grotesque vampiric chupacabra, believing that it can - finally - be categorised within a zoological frame of reference rather than a purely paranormal one. Along the way he uncovers mystery after mystery, has a run in with terrorists, art historians, and even has his garden buzzed by a UFO. By turns both terrifying and funny, this remarkable book is a real tour de force by one of the world's foremost cryptozoological researchers.

DR SHUKER'S CASEBOOK
Dr Karl Shuker - ISBN 978-1905723-33-1

£14.99

Although he is best-known for his extensive cryptozoological researches and publications, Dr Karl Shuker has also investigated a very diverse range of other anomalies and unexplained phenomena, both in the literature and in the field. Now, compiled here for the very first time, are some of the extraordinary cases that he has re-examined or personally explored down through the years.

**CFZ PRESS, MYRTLE COTTAGE,
WOOLFARDISWORTHY BIDEFORD,
NORTH DEVON, EX39 5QR
www.cfz.org.uk**

Other books available from
CFZ PRESS

CFZ PRESS

Dinosaurs and Other Prehistoric Animals on Stamps: A Worldwide Catalogue
Dr Karl P.N.Shuker - ISBN 978-1-905723-34-8

£9.99

Compiled by zoologist Dr Karl P.N. Shuker, a lifelong, enthusiastic collector of wildlife stamps and with an especial interest in those that portray fossil species, it provides an exhaustive, definitive listing of stamps and miniature sheets depicting dinosaurs and other prehistoric animals issued by countries throughout the world. It also includes sections dealing with cryptozoological stamps, dinosaur stamp superlatives, and unofficial prehistoric animal stamps.

CFZ EXPEDITION REPORT 2008 - RUSSIA
ISBN 978-1-905723-35-5

Since 1992, the CFZ has carried out an unparalleled programme of research and investigation all over the world. In July 2008, a five-person team - Richard Freeman, Chris Clarke, Dave Archer, Adam Davies and Keith Townley went to Kabardino-Balkaria in southern Russia in search of the almasty, maybe mankind's closest relative. Here, for the first time, is their story...With an introduction by Jonathan Downes and forward by Dr. Karl Shuker.

CENTRE FOR FORTEAN ZOOLOGY 2009 YEARBOOK
Edited by Jonathan Downes and Richard Freeman
ISBN 978 -1-905723-37

£12.50

The Centre For Fortean Zoology Yearbook is a collection of papers and essays too long and detailed for publication in the CFZ Journal *Animals & Men*. With contributions from both well-known researchers, and relative newcomers to the field, the Yearbook provides a forum where new theories can be expounded, and work on little-known cryptids discussed.

THE MYSTERY ANIMALS OF THE BRITISH ISLES:
KENT
Neil Arnold
ISBN 978-1-905723-36-2

£12.50

Mystery animals? Great Britain? Surely not. But is is true.

This is a major new series from CFZ Press. It will cover Great Britain and the Republic of Ireland, on a county by county basis, describing the mystery animals of the entire island group.

CFZ PRESS, MYRTLE COTTAGE, WOOLFARDISWORTHY BIDEFORD, NORTH DEVON, EX39 5QR
www.cfz.org.uk

Other books available from
CFZ PRESS

GIANT SNAKES
By Michael Newton
ISBN: 978-1-905723-39-3

£9.99

In this exciting book, Michael Newton takes an overview of the most terrifying uberpredators in the world - giant snakes. Outsized examples of known species as well as putative new species are looked at in detail.

THE MYSTERY ANIMALS OF THE BRITISH ISLES: THE WESTERN ISLES
Glen Vaudrey
ISBN 978-1-905723-42-3

£12.50

Mystery animals? Great Britain? Surely not. But is is true.

This is a major new series from CFZ Press. It will cover Great Britain and the Republic of Ireland, on a county by county basis, describing the mystery animals of the entire island group.

Strangely Strange but Oddly Normal
Andy Roberts
ISBN 978-1-905723-44-7

£14.99

An anthology of writings from one of Britain's most respected Fortean authors, covering everything from UFOs, to the Rolling Stones, and from psychedelic drugs to ancient fertility symbols, the Incredible String Band, and government cover-ups.

China: The Yellow Peril?
Richard Muirhead
ISBN 978-1-905723-41-6

£7.99

Richard Muirhead takes an in depth look at the history of Western relationships with China. If some Victorian antiquarians are to be believed contact between the Chinese Empire and other Middle Eastern and Western Empires goes back to times long before the birth of Christ, such as the ancient Egyptians and the Roman Empire.

**CFZ PRESS, MYRTLE COTTAGE,
WOOLFARDISWORTHY BIDEFORD,
NORTH DEVON, EX39 5QR
w w w . c f z . o r g . u k**